ALLIED PHOTO RECONNAISSANCE

OF WORLD WAR TWO

ALLIED PHOTO
RECONNAISSANCE

OF WORLD WAR TWO

Edited by Chris Staerck

THUNDER BAY
P·R·E·S·S

This edition published in 1998 by
Thunder Bay Press
5880 Oberlin Drive, Suite 400
San Diego, California 92121
1-800-284-3580

http://www.admsweb.com

Produced by
PRC Publishing Ltd,
Kiln House, 210 New Kings Road, London SW6 4NZ

ISBN 1 57145 161 7
(or Library of Congress CIP data if available)

1 2 3 4 5 98 99 00 01 02

Printed and bound in China

Acknowledgements
The Editor and Publisher should like to thank the following
for their help in preparing this book:
Michael Sharpe, who wrote the Introduction and the
Conclusion.
Jonathan Falconer, who wrote Chapters 1, 2, 3, and 9.
Norman Franks, who wrote Chapters 4 and 7.
Jerry Scutts, who wrote Chapters 5 and 6.
Chris Staerck, who wrote Chapter 8.
Nick Grant, who wrote Chapters 10 and 11.
Duncan Richey, who wrote Chapter 12.

Roy C. Nesbit, who provided most of the photographs and
caption information for the Introduction.

The Public Records Office was the source of all the
photographs and documents unless specifically credited.

Crown Copyright material in the Public Record Office is
reproduced by the permission of the Controller of Her
Majesty's Stationery Office.

Images are reproduced by courtesy of the Public Record
Office.

Research at Public Record Office undertaken by Chris
Staerck and Hugh Alexander.

ABBREVIATIONS & GLOSSARY

AA	Anti-aircraft
AEAF	Allied Expeditionary Air Force
AOP	Air Observation Post
AVM	Air Vice Marshal
Bar	With medals means a second award: eg DFC and Bar
BEF	British Expeditionary Force
Brig	Brigadier
BG	Bomb Group (USAAF)
BS	Bomb Squadron (USAAF)
Capt	Captain
CIU	Central Interpretation Unit
CO	Commanding Officer
Col	Colonel
cu in	cubic inch
DFC	Distinguished Flying Cross
Dr	Doctor
DSO	Distinguished Service Order
Flg Off	Flying Officer
Flt Lt	Flight Lieutenant
Flt Off	Flight Officer
Flt Sgt	Flight Sergeant
ft	feet
Gen	General
Gp Capt	Group Captain
H2S	A ground-mapping radar
in	inch
JCIU	Joint CIU
lb	pound
Lt-Col	Lieutenant-colonel
MAAF	Mediterranean Allied Air Force
Maj	Major
Met Flt	Meteorological Flight (RAF)
Mk	Mark
MT	Motor Transport
No	Number
NWAPRW	Northwest African PR Wing
Para	Parachute
PFF	Path Finder Force
Plt Off	Pilot Officer
POW	Prisoner of War
PIU	Photographic Interpretation Unit
PR	Photo-reconnaissance
PRS	PR Squadron
PRU	PR Unit
RAAF	Royal Australian Air Force
RAF	Royal Air Force
RCAF	Royal Canadian Air Force
RFC	Royal Flying Corps
RNAS	Royal Naval Air Service
RNZAF	Royal New Zealand Air Force
SAAF	South African Air Force
Sgt	Sergeant
sq in	square inch
Sqn	Squadron (RAF)
Sqn Ldr	Squadron Leader
TacR	Tactical reconnaissance
TAF	Tactical Air Force
TRG	Tactical Reconnaissance Group
TRS	Tactical Reconnaissance Squadron
USAAF/C	US Army Air Force/Corps
Wg Cdr	Wing Commander

Note on Unit Nomenclature
Military units tend to have a preferred method of description which is not always logical. In this book Allied armies are spelled out (US First Army); corps are given Roman numerals (XXXth Corps); divisions, regiments, squadrons, and units use Arabic numerals (16th). RAF, RCAF, RAAF, and SAAF squadrons are identified by their number (No 617).

CONTENTS

Introduction   6

    Early Days   6

    The Twentieth Century   7

    Changing Opinions—World War I   8

    Between the Wars   10

PR Camera Equipment   12

PR Aircraft of World War II   14

1 RAF Operations to stop Operation *"Seelöwe"*—the German invasion of Britain   24

2 The Dambusters Raid—Operation "Chastise"   32

3 The Bombing of Hamburg—Operation "Gomorrah"   42

4 The Channel Dash—Operation "Cerberus"   54

5 The Landings at Salerno—Operation "Avalanche"   62

6 Breaking the Gustav Line—Monte Cassino   70

7 The D-Day landings—Operation "Overlord"   78

8 The Normandy Breakout—Operations "Goodwood" and "Cobra"   90

9 Finding and Destroying the V-Weapons—Operations "Bodyline" & "Crossbow"   98

10 The Advance into Holland—Operation "Market Garden"   110

11 The Rhine Crossing—Operation "Varsity"   120

12 The Liberation of Allied POWs—Operations "Eclipse" and "Exodus"   128

Conclusion   138

    The Luftwaffe Aufklärungsgruppe *v the Allies*   138

    RAF PR—Unarmed and alone   140

    The USAAF Reconnaissance Groups   140

    Photographic Interpretation—Seeing the wood for the trees   140

    The Strategic Bombing Offensive   142

    The Role of PR in propaganda   143

INTRODUCTION

Quite undeservedly, Allied photo-reconnaissance (PR) through the course of World War II has been largely overlooked by aviation historians. There is a tendency to catalogue the minutiae of air-to-air combat and strategic bombing, which is no bad thing, but there is a danger of diminishing the more obscure functions performed by Allied airmen. The importance of PR as a contributing factor to the Allied victory has, therefore, been underplayed.

In fact, it was vital to the war effort and recognized as such by the end of the war. From the spotting of invasion barges in the ports of northern Europe in 1940, through the shadowing of the German capital ships such as *Bismarck* and *Tirpitz*, to the daily information on the targets for Allied day or night bombers, PR assisted the management and direction of Allied forces. Just how important PR was during World War II can be gauged by the detailed analysis in this study of some famous military actions of the war, from the perspective of the role that PR played.

Before looking at World War II PR missions, we shall examine briefly the history of PR up to its position at the beginning of World War II, the principal aircraft operated by the RAF and the USAAF and the range of camera equipment available to them.

Early Days

The first use of aircraft for military purposes was in a reconnaissance role. European military commanders recognized the advantage that could be gained from assessing enemy troop concentrations and formations from the air as early as 1783. During the Franco-Prussian war of 1789, hydrogen balloons were used for artillery spotting with some success. Development was slow, hampered by a lack of funding and disinterest among senior officers. Reconnaissance work was generally accepted as the role of light cavalry units, and military ballooning was viewed as merely an adjunct to their operations.

By the mid-nineteenth century, France had developed a clear lead in the field. Her aviators were the first to take to the air in a powered airship, and the first to begin experimenting with aerial photography. Early methods were crude and often unsatisfactory, but progress continued apace in both France and the United States. Balloons were again used in a tactical role during the American Civil War between 1861 and 1865, and when the Prussians laid siege to Paris in 1870, the French floated vital messages over Prussian lines in manned balloons.

Somewhat belatedly, the British War Office ordered a commission to assess the practical use of balloons to its forces, yet provided little in the way of funds to pursue this research. However, in 1878, British military ballooning received a great boost with the establishment of a dedicated unit at Woolwich in south London. In 1882, the formal School of Ballooning was created at Chatham in Kent, the home of the School of Military Engineering.

The Americans already had considerable experience of military reconnaissance by this stage. John La Mountain, attached to the Rhode Island First Regiment, ascended from a ship off Hampton Roads, Virginia, in August 1861, to observe Confederate batteries positioned to fire on Fort Monroe. His report allowed Union commanders to launch a successful attack that took the batteries completely by surprise, and captured their guns. La Mountain continued to provide the Union with invaluable information until November, when his balloon was lost in high winds.

Undoubtedly the most famous of Civil War balloonists was Thaddeus S. C. Lowe. Lowe was an extremely skilled aviator and an energetic innovator. He developed a system of telegraphic air-to-ground communication and improved aerial photography immeasurably by inventing a photographic enlarger. Prior to his resignation Lowe had made over 3,000 flights for the Union, and despite the fact that he was frustrated by a general misconception of his reconnaissance role, Lowe could perhaps truly be called the father of photo-reconnaissance in the United States armed forces.

During the British war in Sudan from 1885, a unit of military balloons was used in the role of artillery correction. This was seen for many years as the main role of the aerial observer, to look for the fall of shot on enemy positions and to signal the gunners with the adjustments if nec-

The New Naval Airship 'The Baby'

The "Beta"
F. Scovell, Photo No.9

Above: Early photograph of the experimental dirigibles *Baby* and *Beta*, that went to No 1 Company, Air Battalion, Royal Engineers. Their role was artillery spotting and aerial photography. *BPL*

essary. Much of the training carried out at the British Army's School of Ballooning, which moved to Aldershot in 1891, was centered around this perceived role. Airships were still very much in the development stage at this time, although in 1900 the airship pioneer Count Ferdinand von Zeppelin made a number of successful ascents in a rigid framed hydrogen-filled airship, a fact that did not go unnoticed in Washington or London.

The Twentieth Century

The Wright brothers' historic flight in 1903 should have spelled the death knell of the balloon as the primary platform for military observation. However, the adoption of powered fixed-wing aircraft in the United States and Britain was still hampered for some years by official indifference. The French showed a more open-minded approach. They were still smarting from the Franco-Prussian war and enthusiastically embraced any innovation that could restore their military prowess. When Louis Bleriot hopped across the Channel in his tiny Type XI monoplane in 1909, the British military establishment failed to see the significance and continued to focus on lighter-than-air craft and man-carrying kites. The press was more vociferous in its reaction, and expressed grave fears of the possibilities of airborne invasion by gun-toting Frenchmen! H. G. Well's prophetic novel *The War in the Air*, published the previous year, had sowed the germ of fear in the public imagination with a fictional account of vast German

squadrons laying waste to Europe and North America, in believably realistic terms.

When the Air Battalion of the Royal Engineers was formed in April 1911, its primary roles were artillery spotting, reconnaissance, and aerial photography. Very few people perceived the aircraft as a strategic offensive weapon; as a whole military aviation was still very much subservient to ground forces and to their commanders, many of whom were extremely reluctant to give it any credence.

In the United States, military leaders largely failed to capitalize on the advances made by their home-grown aviators. In the Spanish-American War of 1898, aerial reconnaissance had played a vital part in the American victory at the Battle of San Juan Hill. But in the annual maneuvers of 1911, the fact that a lone airman in a fixed-wing aircraft failed to spot the enemy convinced many in the American top brass that military aviation was a waste of money.

Competition between the official Royal Aircraft Factory and private enterprise, and the internal wrangling between the Royal Navy and British Army, continued to hamper the development of British military aviation. In 1912, however, the War Office launched a recruiting drive to encourage new applicants for the Royal Flying Corps, seeking in particular those with

Above: The Royal Naval Air Service used non-rigids for observation and scouting duties. This is C (Coastal) airship No 23. BPL

knowledge of, and experience in, the popular art of photography. There was an explosion in popular photography during the Edwardian era, and the British military leadership was eager to exploit the new found knowledge of the populace for military purposes. The first dedicated unit for aerial photography was based at Farnborough, under the command of Sgt Frederick C. V. Laws. Laws proved to be an influential and dedicated leader of the fledgling unit. He was a keen amateur photographer, and persuaded senior commanders to carry him aloft in their craft to conduct experiments in aerial photography purely on his own initiative. Laws made great strides in aerial mapping; aided by the first camera to be specially developed for air photography in the RFC, the Watson Air Camera, he took aerial photographs of a royal inspection in 1914 of remarkable clarity.

Changing opinions—World War I

At the outbreak of World War I, the British Army was still largely unaware of the advantages to be gained from aerial reconnaissance. Many of its senior officers expressed the belief that gentlemen would never consider the resorting to such tactics on the battlefield. However, as they were soon to find out, the conflict had little to do with chivalry. The full strength of the RFC accompanied the British Expeditionary Force to France in 1914, but Laws found himself seconded to one of the army AA batteries, pointing out friendly aircraft for the inexperienced gunners!

During the fall of 1914, the British began to send up recce aircraft crewed by a pilot and air observer, to observe German troop formations. Photography was still barely considered, and reliance was placed on the written reports of the aerial observers.

It took a clear and detailed map produced from photographs taken from the air by French airmen to convince British high commanders of the tremendous advantage of tactical reconnaissance. On the recommendation of the officer who studied French photographic techniques, an experimental photographic section was set up in the RFC in spring 1915. Under their legendary commander, Lt-Col Hugh Trenchard, the First Wing of the RFC consolidated the most experienced airmen photographers into a single unit and did much to encourage men such as Laws and pioneering aviator John Moore Brabazon in their work. Trenchard was apt to button holing his less enlightened fellow officers by showing them aerial photographs he carried about his person, as evidence of the revolutionary role of PR.

Because of the need to fly continuously along a given heading at a pre-designated height and speed, PR in World War I was a dangerous undertaking. As in any war, the needs of the battle forced a rapid improvement in technology,

Left: PR has always been a dangerous game, and during World War I it quickly became apparent that PR aircraft had to be well defended to survive. Here a mechanic hands over photographic plates to the observer of an RE8 near Arras, February 22, 1918. Better equipped to defend itself than earlier reconnaissance aircraft (note the forward-firing machine gun and the observer's ring-mounted Lewis gun), the camera was mounted vertically. *BPL*

Below: Photographic mosaics of the front line are pieced together, February 1918, two months before the Royal Air Force was formed in April 1918. *BPL*

but aircraft allocated to the reconnaissance units tended to be those rejected by fighter and bomber squadrons. Airships were still in widespread use, particularly by units charged with maritime reconnaissance, but the demands for accurate, up to the minute, aerial photographs had increased enormously. By July 1916, every front-line squadron had its own photographic section.

When the United States entered the war in April 1917, its airmen brought experience of aerial observation in its war against Mexico. During the short course of its involvement in World War I—less than a year—United States reconnaissance units took over 18,000 photographs in support of its gunners in what was an artilleryman's war.

Both sides were all too aware of the important role of PR in the closing years of the conflict, and this made observation planes the target for intensive ground and air attack. The courage of those pioneers is undisputed, and it was they who laid the foundations for others to build on.

Between the wars

As is so often the case in peacetime, in the post-World War I years there was a general failure to capitalize on the hard-won experience of the war years. Interest in military aviation on both sides of the Atlantic declined markedly, and PR was no exception. The type of aircraft employed still tended to be slow and vulnerable, and few pilots seemed interested in this branch of aerial warfare.

Above: Sidney Cotton, an Australian who had flown with the RNAS during World War I, was an enthusiastic supporter of PR and flew his Lockheed 12 around Europe in the inter-war period, photographing areas of military interest with—concealed by sliding panels—three 5in F24 cameras in the fuselage, two Leicas in the wings, and hand-held equipment. The aircraft was painted duck-egg green (he registered this as "Camotint"), the color he thought most suitable for high-altitude camouflage. Here, his aircraft is seen in 1991. *Sergeant G. Dinsdale RAF (Ret'd)*

Trenchard was given the position of Chief of Air Staff in 1919 and despite his emphasis of the importance of photography, it did not receive great priority in RAF planning. The PR aircraft of the RAF did make some highly successful mapping expeditions for British colonies abroad, but little was done to develop cameras and aerial photography, and photographic interpretation was very much the domain of the army.

Alarm bells began to ring in 1937, when a high-level conference of RAF officers was tersely informed that the RAF had a woefully inadequate PR capability. Most of the aircraft dedicated to this role were 1920s vintage biplanes carrying equipment that was generally outmoded.

In 1938, with war becoming an increasingly likelihood, RAF units made invaluable reconnaissance missions to photograph the Italian military build-up in the Mediterranean and Adriatic. Covert missions were flown in a civilian Lockheed 12 to observe the German fleet in the months immediately prior to the war, much to the approval of the Admiralty. The RAF continued, however, to denigrate the role of PR and pass it over to aircraft that were incapable of performing this role satisfactorily—the Blenheim IV, for example, with mediocre speed and ceiling was expected to carry out long-range strategic reconnaissance. Only with the foresight of men such as the Sidney Cotton (whose Lockheed 12 had been used for the overflights of Germany) and Sqn Ldr M. V. Longbottom were RAF photo-reconnaissance units forged into some semblance of operational capability by September 1939, and their guiding and inspirational leadership was to have a profound impact. Cotton was sidelined fairly early in the war by the Air Ministry, who disapproved of his unorthodox methods, yet he was largely responsible for changing official attitudes to the role of the PR in the dusty corridors of power. By the end of 1940 the RAF PR squadrons were equipped with aircraft adequate for the role they were asked to perform. Men and resources were allocated rather belatedly, and specialist training was provided for the photographic interpreters. An important breakthrough in the field of tactical reconnaissance came with the development of mobile processsing units that could be deployed in the field to provide constantly updated information to commanders. Such units were used successfully in Northwest Europe, Italy, North Africa, and the Far East.

American armed forces had also been run down in the aftermath of World War I, and suffered from government spending cuts during the depression era. PR was considered a low priority in defense spending that placed little emphasis on military aviation as a whole. While the Americans developed a formidable strategic bomber during the mid-1930s in the form of the B-17, they had a dearth of effective reconnaissance aircraft. When the Nazis invaded Poland in September 1939, the USAAC suffered from the same official indifference to PR as the RAF. Although a specialized photographic interpretation course was set up in 1939, the principles and techniques of long range (ie, strategic) reconnaissance were misunderstood and underdeveloped. US Observation squadrons, like their British counterparts, were equipped with obsolete machinery, such as the Douglas O-46 and North American O-47.

The transition that these poorly equipped and organized Allied units underwent during World War 2 is remarkable, and a tribute to forward-thinking men and women who flew in the face of official indolence.

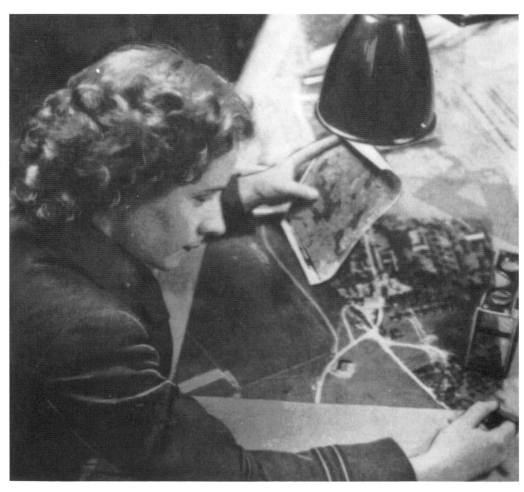

Left: It was during World War II that the interpretation of PR material came of age. Such exponents of the art as Flt Off Constance Babbington Smith played a significant role in identifying secret weapons such as the V-1 and V-2. *Roy C. Nesbit Collection*

PR CAMERA EQUIPMENT

Early camera equipment was bulky and relied on glass plates that were extremely sensitive to the vagaries of the weather. The development of dry plates improved this situation immeasurably in the late nineteenth century, but the first truly significant breakthrough in British PR came with the introduction of the Watson Air Camera in 1913. This device had been developed on the specific advice of Sgt Victor Laws, who recognized the need for vertical photographs for military purposes. Prior to this, most photographs were taken at an oblique angle, making them unsuitable for mapping.

In early 1915 the A-type camera came into service. This could be used in both the oblique and vertical angles. Manufactured by the Thornton-Pickard Manufacturing Company, the photographs it produced were excellent. It was used with great success in the preparations for the battle of Neuve Chapelle in March 1915. It was made from wood, with brass bindings, had an 8.5in lens, and took 5in x 4in plates.

Unacceptable losses of reconnaissance aircraft to anti-aircraft fire led to the development of the LB high-level camera, which had a focal length of up to 20in (51cm). The camera was powered by an air-driven generator and was considerably easier to maintain or operate than its predecessors. An enlarged version known as the BM-type was hampered by its weight and size.

Between the wars, solid progress was made in the development of cameras and film. Ordinary film (which had been introduced at the end of the war) proved sensitive to light at the blue end of the spectrum, and panochromatic film was invented in response. Infra-red film was developed that could record objects clearly over great distances, while cameras grew even larger to give better and sharper images from greater altitudes. Multi-lens cameras were invented that could give all-round coverage, or to provide one vertical and two oblique images. In 1925, the Royal Aircraft Establishment produced the F24, which became the mainstay of RAF photographic units until the end of World War II. It was a highly reliable piece of kit, but not really suited to its role, lacking the definition required at high altitude. In various guises, such as an increased lens size and focal length, this camera remained in use throughout the war.

The standard US cameras were the K-17, the K-22 and the K-24. The F-6 version of the P-38 was usually equipped with either a K-22 with a 12in cone for vertical photography from an altitude of up to 6,000ft, or the K-17 with a 6in lens for operations at half that altitude. American tactical reconnaissance aircraft perfoming low altitude oblique photography missions were often equipped with a K-24 camera mounted at an oblique angle. These low-level oblique photographs were particularly useful as a tactical asset to fighter-bomber pilots in Northwest Europe. High altitude photography between 20-40,000ft was achieved with installation of K-14 and K-22 cameras with lenses of up to 40in. For night reconnaissance a device called the D-2 Flash unit was used. It was based on a K-19 or K-29 camera and was operated at a height of 2-3,000ft. The D-2 synchronized with a powerful Edgerton lamp that could deliver 200,000,000 candelpower intensity every three seconds.

Above Right: World War I PR—a C-type camera is adjusted by a mechanic. It's fitted to a BE2c biplane. *BPL*

Below Right: The mainstay of RAF photographic units during World War II was the F24 camera, which came into service in 1925. It could be both hand-held or used in a fixed position, was highly reliable, and would see service for over 30 years. It had a number of lens options and used roll film. *Roy C. Nesbit Collection*

Below: The American K-20 was used as a hand-held camera for daytime reconnaissance. It had a 63/8in lens and could shoot a roll film of 50 exposures. *John K. Nesbit via Roy C. Nesbit*

PR AIRCRAFT OF WWII

Although it started the war using the Blenheim IV, it wasn't long before the RAF began to use more suitable machines in the PR role—the Spitfire and Hurricane. Later the all-wooden Mosquito would prove an excellent PR platform, as would the specialized variants of the Lockheed P-38 Lightning and North American P-51 Mustang the USAAF brought with it to Europe in 1942. This brief pictorial survey looks at a range of aircraft used by the Allies for PR during World War II.

Above Right: The Spitfire PR ID was a modified Mk V and entered service in October 1940. It carried two F24 or F8 cameras. *Jim Muncie via Roy C. Nesbit*

Center Right: A rarity—this Spitfire PR IE had two cameras in the wings pointed outward for low level photography. *Roy C. Nesbit collection*

Below Right: The Spitfire PR Mk XI came into service in 1942 and continued with the RAF until the post-war years. *Roy C. Nesbit collection*

Below: Two photographs of early PR Spitfires—IBs—both of No 212 Squadron in France before the Phoney War got real. *Roy C. Nesbit Collection (Below), Jack H. Eggleston via Roy C. Nesbit (Bottom)*

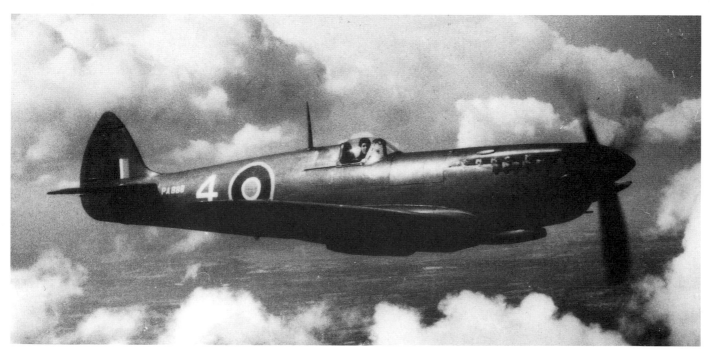

Above: The Blenheim IV was the principal long-range reconnaissance aircraft of the RAF in 1939. Lacking adequate performance for the role a large number of Blenheims were lost in the opening months of the war during daylight missions over Germany. The aircraft was gradually withdrawn from photo-reconnaissance duties. *Roy C. Nesbit Collection*

Right and Below Right: The Liberator was used by Coastal Command to close the "Atlantic Gap," where before U-boats had been able to operate without fear of aerial attack. The F-7 version of the B-24 Liberator was a dedicated photo-reconnaissance aircraft that saw limited service in both European and Pacific theaters. *Both: Roy C. Nesbit Collection*

Above and Below: In RAF service the Consolidated PBY-5 was known as the Catalina Mk I. It had a very long range, made an excellent reconaissance platform, and served with No 210 Squadron based at Sullom Voe in the Shetland Islands. These two photographs show a Mk IVA (Above) and a Mk IB in Scottish waters. *Roy C. Nesbit Collection; BPL*

Above: The de Havilland Mosquito—the "Mozzie"—was one of the finest PR platforms of the conflict. Light, fast, and with a ceiling beyond most fighters sent to intercept it, it was ideally suited to PR. This is a PR Mk XVI with invasion stripes on its wings. *Roy C. Nesbit Collection*

Below: Introduced into RAF service in November 1940, the Handley Page Halifax was the unsung hero of Bomber Command. A Srs Ia version of the aircraft was the first to carry H2S ground-mapping radar, which improved bombing accuracy immeasurably. This is Mk III. *BPL*

Top: Although less numerous than the Spitfire or Mustang, the PR variants of the Hawker Hurricane did valuable service in the Middle East and East Asian theaters. They were much cruder machines than the PR Spitfires, lacking the heating, range, and refinement of the former aircraft. *BPL*

Above: One of the many Allied aircraft that was used in a dual role, the Hawker Typhoon was ostensibly an extremely formidable ground-attack aircraft. Many were fitted with camera equipment during the Allied offensive in Northwestern Europe to assess the effects of attacks on German supply columns. *BPL*

Left: The Hudson was developed from a pre-war airliner, and saw extensive action with both Coastal Command and the USAAF, particularly as a long-range maritime reconnaissance platform. This Hudson is seen over Dunkirk. *BPL*

Below: The potent Lockheed P-38 family spawned two highly successful photo-reconnaissance variants, the F-4 and F-5. Many hundreds were built during the course of the war. This F-5 is being worked on by mechanics of 8th Air Force's 7th Photographic Group. *Dr Eric V. Hawkinson via Roy C. Nesbit*

Right: F-5 Lightning and PR Spitfire. *Dr Eric V. Hawkinson via Roy C. Nesbit*

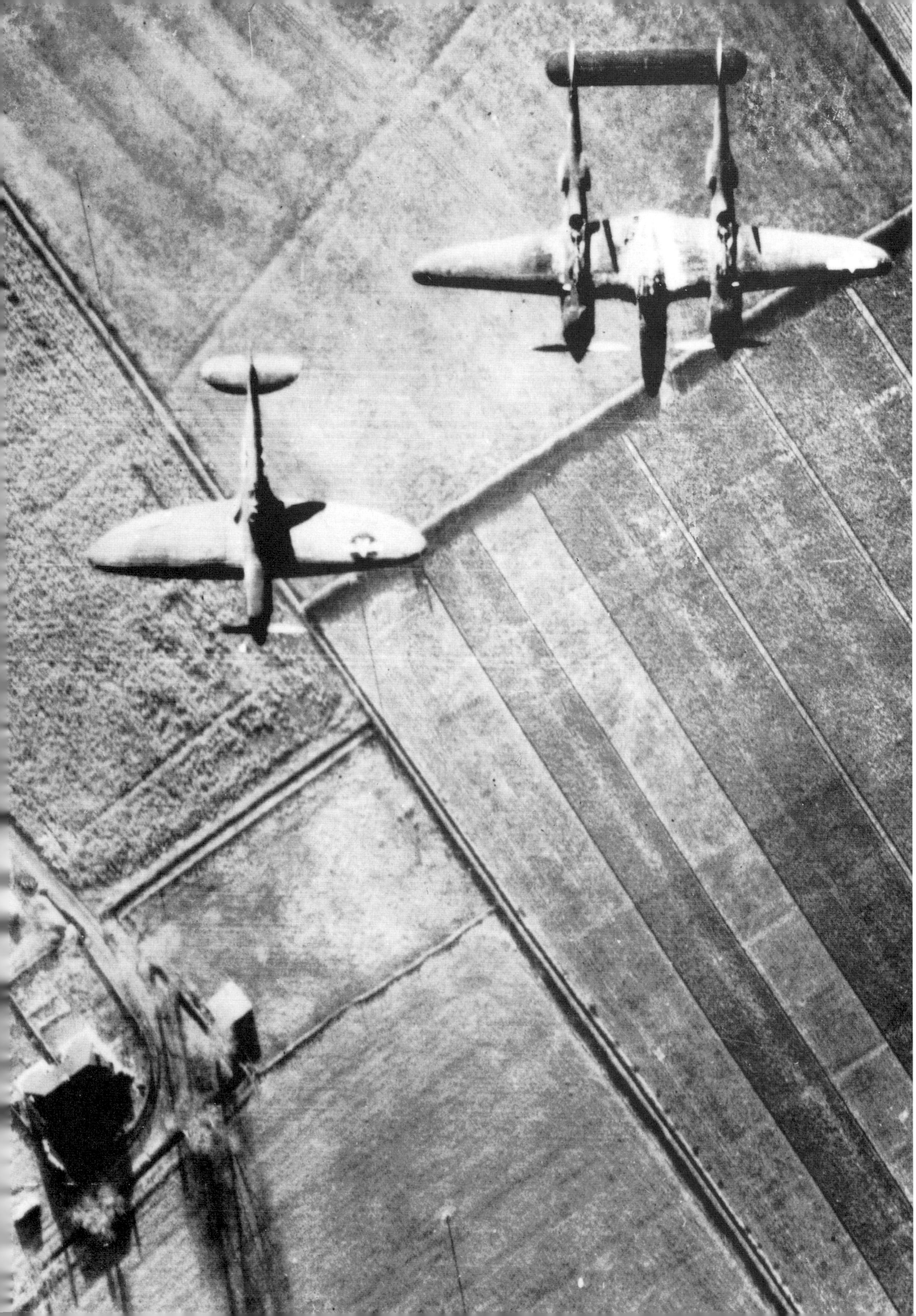

Above: For many the finest fighter aircraft of the war, the North American P-51 Mustang family included a dedicated PR version, the F-6. The Mustang was a classic fighter and was particularly successful as a long-range escort. Four variants of the F-6, the B, C, D, and K were used. Unlike the P-38, they retained full armament. *Roy C. Nesbit Collection*

Below: Early model P-51 over south England. *BPL*

Left: The Short Sunderland was a mainstay of Coastal Command for the duration of the war. As well as providing maritime reconnaissance and escorting convoys, the heavily-armed Sunderland successfully attacked and sunk a number of U-boats. U-boat crews christened it the "Flying Porcupine." *Roy C. Nesbit Collection*

Below Left: Convoy Duty for this Sunderland. *BPL*

Below: The Westland Lysander was introduced into RAF service as a tactical reconnaissance aircraft in May 1938. Although subsequently withdrawn from this role, it gave good service as a liaison and light transport aircraft.. In the foreground is a Lysander Mk III of No 400 (AC) Squadron at Odiham, England. *BPL*

OPERATION "SEELÖWE"

1 RAF OPERATIONS TO STOP OPERATION "*SEELÖWE*" (SEALION)—THE GERMAN INVASION OF BRITAIN IN 1940

MISSION AIM

To bomb and destroy the German invasion fleet massing in the Channel and North Sea ports, waiting to carry troops across the narrow English Channel for an amphibious assault on the south coast of England in the high summer of 1940.

BACKGROUND

In the spring of 1940 the victorious German Army was poised on the brink of the total conquest of Europe. Its Blitzkrieg had swept all aside who had dared stand in its way—Norway had fallen in April, Belgium and Holland in May, and France sued for peace on June 17. By June 3, most of the tattered remnants of the BEF had been plucked from the beaches of Dunkirk by an armada of Allied ships big and small, and the last RAF squadrons based in France withdrew by the 18th. All that stood now between Hitler's armies and the invasion of Britain was the English Channel and the Royal Air Force.

Above: Oil tanks burn in the docklands area of Dunkirk, June 3, 1940. In a fighting retreat before the relentless advance of the German army, the BEF and elements of the French and Belgian armies found themselves hemmed into a small pocket on the beaches of Dunkirk at the end of May 1940.

Right: Weary troops adrift on a lifeboat off the Belgian coast, possibly survivors of a rescue vessel sunk by enemy action in the Channel, photographed with a hand-held camera by the observer of an RAF aircraft.

Below: In this oblique view showing a stretch of the beach at Dunkirk on June 3, 1940, most of the BEF had already been successfully evacuated but some 30,000 French troops were still to be embarked. An improvised pier made from abandoned vehicles can be seen (right) to enable troops to board small ships laying off the beaches, some of which can be seen in the foreground.

To achieve its objective, first the Luftwaffe needed to seize control of the skies over England from the RAF, and then to ship its armies across the Channel to make landings on its southern shores. The invasion fleet comprised largely of hundreds of motorized barges normally used for the movement of freight along the inland waterways of northern Europe, supplemented by hundreds of merchant vessels.

During the period of the Battle of Britain between July 15 and October 31, the main actions were fought by the squadrons of Fighter Command, but for anti-invasion measures the squadrons of Bomber Command acted in a supporting role, launching a prolonged series of attacks against concentrations of enemy invasion shipping wherever and whenever required.

In the opening phases of these attacks, operations were flown mainly in daylight by Bristol Blenheim light bombers of No 2 Group, but as the need to thwart Hitler's invasion plans became ever more crucial, the RAF's medium and heavy bombers were used in greater numbers, mainly by night. Vickers Wellingtons of No 3 Group, Armstrong-Whitworth Whitleys of No 4 Group, and Handley Page Hampdens of No 5 Group flew from their respective airfields in Cambridgeshire and East Anglia, Yorkshire, and Lincolnshire, for the short flight across the Channel or further afield to the North Sea ports. Two Blenheim squadrons from No 2 Group had been detached to Lossiemouth in Scotland to repel invasion forces from Norway, should they come.

Above: Dense black smoke from bombed oil tanks obscured the sky for much of the evacuation period. Here a Lockheed Hudson of RAF Coastal Command overflies the Dunkirk coastline on May 29, the fourth of the 10-day evacuation that saw more than 300,000 troops rescued and brought home to England.

Extensive photo-reconnaissance sorties were flown by Spitfires of No 1 PRU from their base at Heston in Middlesex and were vital in locating and monitoring the ports in which invasion shipping was massing. Reconnaissance flights over the Channel ports were also flown from late July by Blenheims of No 2 Group to augment the sorties of No 1 PRU, and supported on occasions by aircraft from Coastal Command.

THE COURSE OF THE BATTLE

The first PRU sorties to investigate rumors of an invasion fleet gathering in European ports were flown on July 3 and 4, 1940, from the forward operating base at Wick in the north of Scotland. Although the pilots found little of interest, on July 3 a small force of Blenheims bombed the quaysides on the Rhine near Rotterdam where barges were moored.

In the weeks that followed, intelligence sources indicated the Germans were assembling a large naval force south of Trondheim in Norway, but once again photo-reconnaissance showed nothing untoward. However, sorties flown along the coastlines of the Low Countries and France began to show telltale signs of the construction of long range coastal guns on the French coast in the Pas-de-Calais area that might be used to support an amphibious assault on England. But there was still no sign of invasion shipping massing in the Channel ports.

It was important that the potential concentration areas were watched, regardless of the weather conditions, and this meant that when high-level photography was impossible, the PR pilots were sent in at low level. Additional reconnaissance continued to be undertaken by Blenheims of Coastal Command and by aircraft of No 2 Group on missions to Germany.

Then, on September 1, came the first signs of serious invasion preparations by the Germans. Photographs brought back from a PR sortie flown by Flg Off Bill Wise, showed an increasing number of barges moored in the South Beveland and Ternuezen-Ghent Canals, and in the harbor at Hansweert, and the numbers continued to mount over the next two days. Further sorties revealed that the barges were on the move and had passed through the canals to be moored in the Channel ports. Each new cover by PRU Spitfires flying from Heston confirmed that the enemy was moving his vessels into a position to strike. The biggest concentrations were to be found at Ostend, and at Flushing, Dunkirk, Calais, and Boulogne which were promptly singled out for attack by RAF aircraft.

Up until then, Bomber Command's attentions had been sporadic but on the night of September 7/8 the Channel ports of Ostend and Boulogne received the full weight of a concerted attack by more than 80 aircraft, but the atrocious weather conditions experienced on this raid meant that some crews were unable to find their target. On the following night a mixed force of 133 Blenheims, Hampdens, Wellingtons, and

Below: Photo-reconnaissance detected large numbers of invasion barges massing in the Channel ports during September 1940. Bomber Command was called upon to attack and destroy them. Here is a post-raid reconnaissance cover of Dunkirk, bombed on September 19, by Bristol Blenheims of No 82 Squadron, showing sunk and damaged barges and demolished dockyard infrastructure.

Whitleys were despatched to bomb the German North Sea ports of Hamburg, Bremen, and Emden, and the Channel ports of Ostend and Boulogne. The weather over Ostend was bad again and it forced some crews to return home in frustration, having failed to identify their target, but thankfully those crews raiding Bremen fared better. Five Blenheims and two Wellingtons were lost attacking Ostend and Boulogne, and one was missing from the Hamburg raid.

Tension at home was mounting as the number of barges continued to grow steadily in the ports nearest Britain, joined by shoals of E-boats and other small craft. While the nation was put on alert of imminent invasion, the RAF's photographic interpretation unit at Wembley, in north London, watched feverishly for signs that the invasion fleet was putting to sea, and the Heston

Spitfires continued to keep the Channel ports under constant surveillance. Meanwhile, Bomber Command mounted attacks against invasion shipping by day and night, raiding ports in France, Belgium and Germany, and the German heavy guns at Haringzelle, Framzelle, and Cap Gris Nez.

In mid-September extensive photo-reconnaissance coverage by Spitfires of the Channel ports, Antwerp and, further afield, the principal German port of Hamburg (where earlier in July the liners *Europa* and *Bremen* were being prepared for Operation *"Seelöwe"*), showed that the enemy was poised to strike. There were over 1,000 barges in the Channel ports, with at least 600 more at the Belgian port of Antwerp and several hundred merchant vessels capable of supporting an invasion force directed at England. It seemed that Germany was ready to launch its feared invasion.

On September 15 came the climax of the daylight phase of the Battle of Britain when Spitfires and Hurricanes of Fighter Command shot down

Below: The effect of RAF bombing attacks on the port of Le Havre can be seen from the vertical reconnaissance cover, with hits encircled.

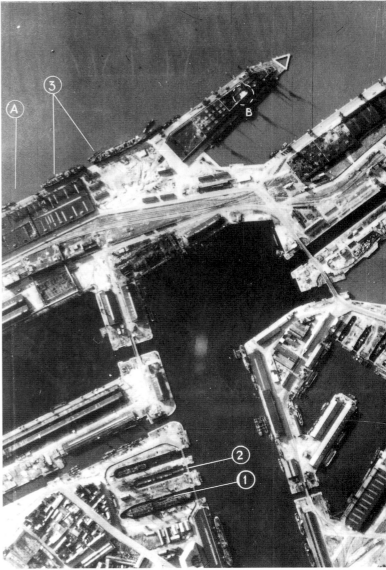

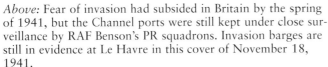

Above: Fear of invasion had subsided in Britain by the spring of 1941, but the Channel ports were still kept under close surveillance by RAF Benson's PR squadrons. Invasion barges are still in evidence at Le Havre in this cover of November 18, 1941.

Above Right and Far Right: Although Hitler was firmly committed to the Eastern Front when this cover was taken of Rotterdam by the RAF in March 1942, there is clear photographic evidence of troop landing craft and barges.

56 German aircraft in a day of pitched air battles in the skies over southern England. The RAF lost 27 aircraft but 14 of the pilots were safe. Unbeknown to Britain, the German High Command had already started to abandon its plans for the invasion of England, but Bomber Command's assault against invasion shipping continued unabated.

On the night of September 15/16 Bomber Command flew 155 sorties, most of them directed against the Channel ports. Shipping in the Belgian port of Antwerp received a pounding and it was during this attack that Bomber Command's second Victoria Cross of the war was won by 18-year-old Sergeant John Hannah, the wireless operator of a No 83 Squadron Hampden. His aircraft was hit by light flak over the port and set on fire, but Hannah chose to stay with the burning aircraft and succeeded in extinguishing the blaze, enabling his pilot to fly the aircraft home to a successful landing in England. Hannah suffered serious burns as the result of his selfless act of bravery.

Bombing operations continued by day on the 16th and 17th, but on the night of the 17th/18th, in the biggest raid of the war so far, Bomber Command despatched a large force of bombers against invasion shipping and targets in Germany. Some two-thirds of the 194 aircraft bombed barges in the Channel ports and only one aircraft was lost from this raid. The Channel ports were then raided virtually every night until the end of the month by Bomber Command.

But at the beginning of October, PR began to show a gradual decrease in the number of barges

and shipping in the Channel ports, and by the end of the month this trend revealed the number of barges had dropped to well below half the figure at the peak in September. Close analayis of photographs by skilled interpreters showed the level of activity on the quaysides had decreased and the barges were now moored side by side parallel with the quays—the more usual position for commercial barges. Meanwhile, in the clear blue skies over southern England the Luftwaffe had been decisively beaten by the pilots of Fighter Command in its attempt to gain air superiority over mainland Britain, the prerequisite for launching its amphibious assault on Britain. Luftwaffe losses during the battle totalled 1,733, the RAF's 915. The RAF raid on enemy shipping in the Channel ports by 24 Blenheims and six Battles on October 12/13 marked the last of the major raids against these targets during the invasion threat period.

The invasion scare was almost over, but fears were voiced about a German invasion fleet massing in the Baltic. On October 29, Flg Off S. J. Millen flew the new Spitfire PR1D (the first true recce version of the Spitfire rather than a conversion from the fighter) over the Baltic and northwest German ports in the longest PR sortie of the war so far. What he photographed set British minds at rest since there was little evidence of a cross-Channel invasion force build-up. Fears of invasion could at last be set aside as the second winter of the war closed in. Meanwhile, in Berlin, Hitler had already begun to turn his attentions to a war in the East against Russia.

PERFORMANCE

Despite the problems caused on occasions by poor weather conditions, Bomber Command largely succeeded in its task of finding and bombing the concentrations of enemy invasion shipping holed up in the Channel ports and further afield. While Fighter Command battled by day from mid-July to early October to deny the Luftwaffe air superiority of the skies over England—vital for a successful amphibious assault—the squadrons of Bomber Command smashed the means by which its armies were to be carried across the English Channel in a sustained bombing campaign. It was a classic example of cooperation between the RAF's Fighter and Bomber Commands.

The role of photo-reconnaissance in bringing about this result was vital, providing up-to-the minute intelligence for the planners at Bomber Command HQ to act upon and send the bombers where they were needed most, and providing post-raid intelligence to confirm the results and if necessary, revisit a target. The strategic success of RAF operations to confound Operation "Seelöwe" was plain, since Hitler called off his invasion plans, although there is evidence to suggest that he had already lost interest by midsummer.

UNITS INVOLVED

RAF Bomber Command front-line Squadrons 1940

No 1 Group, HQ: Hucknall, Notts
12 Sqn Wellington II
103 Sqn Wellington I
142 Sqn Wellington II
150 Sqn Wellington I
300 Sqn Wellington I
301 Sqn Wellington I
304 Sqn Wellington I
305 Sqn Wellington

No 2 GROUP, HQ: Castlewood House, Huntingdon
15 Sqn Blenheim IV
18 Sqn Blenheim IV
21 Sqn Blenheim IV
40 Sqn Blenheim IV
57 Sqn Blenheim IV
82 Sqn Blenheim IV
101 Sqn Blenheim IV
105 Sqn Blenheim IV
107 Sqn Blenheim IV
110 Sqn Blenheim IV
114 Sqn Blenheim IV
139 Sqn Blenheim IV
218 Sqn Blenheim IV

No 3 Group, HQ: Mildenhall, Suffolk
7 Sqn Stirling I
9 Sqn Wellington I
15 Sqn Wellington I
37 Sqn Wellington I
38 Sqn Wellington I
40 Sqn Wellington I
75 Sqn Wellington I
99 Sqn Wellington I
115 Sqn Wellington I
149 Sqn Wellington I
214 Sqn Wellington I
311 Sqn Wellington I

No 4 Group, HQ: Linton-on-Ouse, Yorks
10 Sqn Whitley IV,V
35 Sqn Halifax I
51 Sqn Whitley IV,V
58 Sqn Whitley V
77 Sqn Whitley V
78 Sqn Whitley IVa,V
102 Sqn Whitley V

No 5 Group, HQ: St Vincent's, Grantham, Lincs
44 Sqn Hampden
49 Sqn Hampden
50 Sqn Hampden
61 Sqn Hampden
83 Sqn Hampden
106 Sqn Hampden
144 Sqn Hampden
207 Sqn Manchester I

RAF PR Units 1940
Photographic Development Unit (Jan-July 1940)
Renamed Photographic Reconnaissance Unit (July 1940)
Renamed No 1 Photographic Reconnaissance Unit (Nov 1940)
Lockheed 12a, Spitfire PRI, Hudson I, Blenheim IV

Right: The old and the new threat, Dunkirk, April 1942. At the top of this photograph can be seen the concentrations of barges that had been earmarked for Operation "Seelöwe" in the summer of 1940; at the bottom (indicated A) are U-boat pens under construction, an indication of the serious new threat to Britain's transatlantic supply lines.

OPERATION "CHASTISE"

2 THE DAMBUSTERS RAID
MAY 16/17, 1943

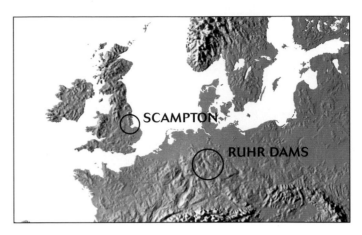

MISSION AIM

To destroy the great dams of the Ruhr—the Mohne, Eder and Sorpe—using a revolutionary "bouncing bomb," to cause widespread disruption by flooding to communications and industry in the Ruhr valley.

BACKGROUND

On March 17, 1943, Squadron "X" was formed in great secrecy with the specific task of breaching the Ruhr dams. Reports from the British Government's Ministry of Economic Warfare had predicted widespread chaos in the Ruhr valley if these dams that provided power for German industry were destroyed. The one major difficulty in achieving this end was that the dam walls were resistant to damage from conventional freefall bombs. Therefore, a means had to be found wherby a sufficiently powerful weapon could be delivered and exploded against a dam wall in such away as to cause a catastrophic breach of the structure.

Ten days later the squadron acquired its specific identity as No 617 Squadron. Most of its 133 aircrew were hand-picked from existing squadrons in No 5 Group by the new commanding officer, Wg Cdr Guy Gibson, DSO and Bar, DFC and Bar. The mix of crews was truly international, with 90 from the RAF, 29 RCAF, 12 RAAF, and two RNZAF. Contrary to popular belief, not all were battle-hardened veterans. Some had flown two tours of ops, many had not completed a first tour, and some were freshman with little more than a handful of ops to their credit.

A modified version of the four-engined Lancaster, the BI (Special), was produced to carry the specially-designed "bouncing bomb," of which more later. To enable the bomb to be carried, the Lancaster's mid-upper turret was removed and faired-over, the bomb doors in the belly of the fuselage were also removed and in

Left: Wg Cdr Guy Gibson's Lancaster BI (Special), ED932-G, showing the "Upkeep" rotating mine in place beneath the fuselage. It is held between a pair of side-swing callipers and rotated, via a belt drive, by a hydraulic motor mounted in the forward fuselage.

Top and Above: Two views of the modified Lancaster BI (Special), ED825-T, showing the faired-over mid-upper gun turret position and the recess in the belly of the fuselage to accommodate the "bouncing bomb," in place of the conventional bomb-bay doors. This aircraft was flown on the dams raid by the American pilot Flt Lt McCarthy.

their place a recess was created into which the bouncing bomb was held between a pair of side-swing V-shaped calliper arms. Power to spin the cylindrical bomb was transferred via a belt-drive from a variable-gear hydraulic motor mounted in the floor of the fuselage, and attached to one side of the weapon.

For some time now, a British inventor named Dr Barnes Wallis had been working on the problem of how to breach the dams. After exhaustive research he had hit upon the idea of a "bouncing bomb" that could be dropped from an aircraft and skipped across the surface of a dam's reservoir, in much the same way as a flat pebble can be made to skim across the surface of water. Codenamed "Upkeep," his bouncing bomb is more accurately described as a spherical air-dropped mine. Rotating at 500 rpm it had to be dropped onto the reservoir from a very low level some 1,200-1,500ft from the dam face. Skipping over anti-torpedo nets it would bounce across the surface of the water until it made contact with the dam wall. Sinking to a predetermined

depth, three hydrostatic pistols would detonate, exploding the main charge of 6,600lb of Torpex explosive against the inner wall of the dam, setting up shock waves that would crack open the structure and allowing the pressure of millions of gallons of water to finish the job and spill out into the valley below.

Photo-reconnaissance was vital to the success of Operation "Chastise." It provided important information to Bomber Command's planners about when the water levels in the reservoirs behind the dams had reached their highest, thereby achieving their maximum flood damage potential. It also gave important up-to-date intelligence on whether anti-aircraft defenses had been strengthened on the dams themselves.

Above: Twenty-four-year-old Wg Cdr Guy Gibson (center), pictured here when CO of No 106 Squadron in early 1943, was chosen to form and lead No 617 Squadron on the epic dams raid on May 16/17, 1943.

Below: This diagram shows how back-spin enabled Barnes Wallis's "bouncing bomb" to skip across the surface of a dam reservoir (A, B, C), over torpedo nets (P, Q), and slide down the inner wall of the dam (E) where the bomb was detonated by hydrostatic pistols.

Below Right: From reconnaissance photographs like this one taken by PR Spitfires from RAF Benson, staff of the CIU, Medmenham, were able to build scale models of the dams to be attacked, in order to help in the raid planning. The Mohne dam, holding back 353,760,000 US gal of water, is pictured here on April 5, 1943, photographed by a Spitfire of No 541 Squadron. Compare this photograph with the post-raid images on page 37 to see the effects of the breaching of the dam.

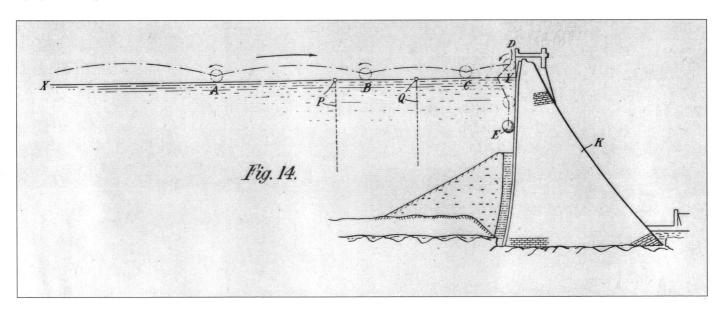

Fig. 14.

THE COURSE OF THE BATTLE

On February 7, 1943, the first of a series of nine photo-reconnaissance sorties were flown by Spitfires of No 541 Squadron from Benson in Oxfordshire to the Mohne dam and its reservoir. When full the Mohne reservoir contained some 140 million tons of water and was the principal source of supply for the industries of the Ruhr valley 20 miles away. The weather was not kind to the recce pilots and it was not until the seventh attempt on February 19 that anything vaguely useful as intelligence was obtained from the photographic coverage. It took two further sorties, the last completed on April 4, to provide photographs of sufficient quality for the Model Section at the CIU Medmenham to build a scale model of the dam and surrounding landscape with which to brief Gibson and his Lancaster crews. The same PR pilots flew most of the sorties over the Ruhr dams. The intention was that they would get to know the dams and their hinterland so well that when they overflew them after the planned attacks they would be able to notice changes in the landscape made by the flood waters.

Meanwhile, the crews of No 617 Squadron trained intensively for six weeks, practicing low-level flying by day and night to improve navigation skills and build confidence in flying safely over water at low-level. Practice attacks were made over Uppingham and Derwent reservoirs to help perfect their bombing technique before the actual operation itself.

In early April a request was made for photographic coverage of the Eder and Sorpe dams, which lay some 50 miles southeast and 6 miles southwest respectively of the Mohne. The Eder was even bigger than the Mohne, containing more than 200 million tons of water. The reconnaissance was completed on the afternoon of May and in the morning of the 15th by Spitfire PR XIs of No 542 Squadron. By mid-afternoon on May 15 the results of these recce flights and the intelligence interpretations were ready. Once again detailed scale models were built of the dams and the surrounding landscape to help the bomber crews. Just in case the enemy got wind of the impending operation, the PR pilots were briefed to cover a variety of targets in the Ruhr valley and across Holland in the same sortie so as not to draw undue attention to their real interest.

The first Type 464 Provisioning Lancaster BI (Special) arrived at Scampton on April 8, with the final aircraft being delivered on May 16. On May 11-12 the crews who were to fly the operation practiced dropping inert-filled "Upkeep" cylinders along the north Kent coast at Reculver, and a full dress-rehearsal by all 19 Lancasters was flown on the night of May 14 at Eyebrook reservoir (Uppingham) and Colchester's Abberton reservoir in Essex. On the afternoon of May 15, No 5 Group received the order from HQ Bomber Command to execute Operation "Chastise"—the dams were to be attacked on the night of May 16/17.

Not until the main briefing for the operation were the crews finally notified on their targets after months of guesswork of their part (the favorite was a precision attack on the battleship *Tirpitz*)—the six dams in western Germany, located to east and southeast of the Ruhr. Nineteen Lancasters were to fly in three waves, the first comprising nine aircraft led by Wg Cdr Guy Gibson, their target the Mohne dam. If that dam was successfully breached, any aircraft whose mines had not been dropped were to fly on to attack the Eder dam. The second wave of five Lancasters led by Flt Lt J. C. McCarthy, an American, was actually to take-off first and fly singly by way of a more northerly route to bomb the Sorpe dam. A third, reserve, wave of five

Lancasters led by Plt Off W. H. T. Ottley, was to take off two hours later and attack the last resort targets—the Diemel, Ennepe and Lister dams—but if the three main target dams had not been breached they would be called upon to attack them.

Shortly before 21.30hrs on the evening of May 16, the first of 19 Lancasters took off from Scampton in three waves, each carrying a bouncing bomb beneath its belly. They headed at low level across the North Sea and crossed the Dutch coast before making their way inland towards the Ruhr. One aircraft had already returned early after it struck the sea in a glancing blow that ripped off its bomb (Plt Off G. Rice in "AJ-H"). Five more aircraft were shot down or crashed on the way to the target—Plt Off V. W. Byers ("AJ-K"), Flt Lt W. Astell ("AJ-B"), Plt Off L. J. Burpee ("AJ-S"), Flt Lt R. N. G. Barlow ("AJ-E"), and Plt Off W. H. T. Ottley ("AJ-C"). One more was badly holed by flak (Flt Lt J. L. Munro in "AJ-W"), causing it to turn for home without bombing.

Out of an initial force of 19 aircraft, this left 12 Lancasters to bomb the dams.

Amidst intense flak, Wg Cdr Guy Gibson and four more crews bombed the Mohne dam and

Right and Below: Intelligence gathering did not stop at aerial reconnaissance. This German scale map of the Mohne Dam and surrounding countryside, and a pre-war photograph of the dam itself, were probably obtained from an Air Ministry appeal early in the war for maps and photographs of locations in Germany that could be used for intelligence purposes.

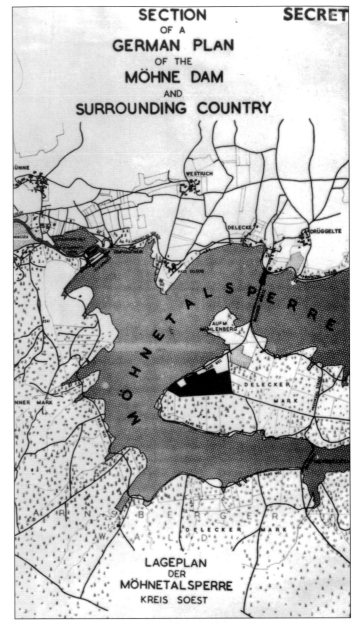

succeeded in breaching its walls on the fourth attempt, with Flt Lt D. J. H. Maltby's aircraft ("AJ-J") making the vital breach that caused the wall to burst. Gibson then proceeded to fly the 40 miles to bomb the Eder dam, accompanied by Flt Lt D. J. Shannon ("AJ-L"), Sqn Ldr H. E. Maudslay ("AJ-Z"), Plt Off L. G. Knight ("AJ-N") and Sqn Ldr H. M. Young ("AJ-A"). Thankfully, the dam was undefended but due to its geographical location proved more difficult to bomb than the Mohne. After some 10 attempts the Eder dam was spectacularly breached by Knight's Lancaster. The Lancasters of Flt Lt J. C McCarthy ("AJ-T") and Flt Sgt K. W. Brown ("AJ-F") bombed the Sorpe dam, but without success and the walls remained intact. The twelfth Lancaster piloted by Flt Sgt C. T. Anderson ("AJ-Y") was unable to find its target and returned to base without dropping its mine. The three Lancasters shot down after making their attacks were those of Maudslay, Young, and Flt Lt J. V. Hopgood ("AJ-M").

Only 11 aircraft returned to Scampton as dawn was breaking—eight failed to return and 53 crew were killed, making it a costly operation in terms of men and aircraft. For his bravery in leading the raid and for drawing the attention of the defending flak gunners away from subsequent attacks by his pilots, Gibson was awarded the Victoria Cross. Thirty-four other aircrew received decorations for the parts they had played in the successful prosecution of the raid.

So that photographic coverage could be obtained as early as possible on the morning after the attack, the CO of No 542 Squadron was informed by Bomber Command HQ of the exact time of the attack so he could arrange for a recce aircraft to be over the targets at first light. The first PR Spitfire took off from Benson at 07.30hrs and arrived high over the Ruhr to be greeted by the industrial haze from its myriad factories. But away to the east the skies were clear and the huge floods caused by the breaches in the Mohne and Eder dams were plain to see from 30,000ft as they coursed their way through

MOEHNE DAM
(After attack)
K 1559
Neg. Nº 24686

Right: A Spitfire PR IX flown by Flg Off Jerry Fray of No 542 Squadron was over the Ruhr at first light on May 17 to obtain the first dramatic photographic coverage of the breached dams. In this sequence of photographs, water can be seen pouring through the large breach in the Mohne dam (*Top and Center*) while 13 miles downstream in the Ruhr Valley at Frondenberg (*Right*) the flood waters have covered roads, railway lines, and bridges.

the valley. The Spitfire PR IX flown by Flg Off Jerry Fray made several runs over the targets and obtained good clear photographs. That same day two further sorties were despatched from Benson to photograph the breaches in two of the dams, and to record the devastation caused as unrelenting torrents of water released from behind them cascaded down into the valleys below, sweeping all before them. Photo-reconnaissance revealed that the damage in the valley below the Eder dam was far worse than that downstream from the Mohne.

PERFORMANCE

Breaching the Mohne and Eder dams was a huge achievement. The millions of gallons of water that poured forth from out of the breached walls inundated nearly 40 miles of valleys and caused the deaths of more than 1,300 people. Steel production in the factories of the Ruhr was affected for the remainder of the year, pumping stations became silted up by the flood water, roads, railways, and canals were severely disrupted, and agriculture and food supplies suffered from the flooding. Had the Sorpe dam also been breached, the repercussions for Ruhr industry and civilians living close by would have been catastrophic. At home, the morale of the British people received a boost when it heard of this major feat of arms. To the RAF and Dr Barnes Wallis the success of the raid represented major triumphs in airmanship and technology, respectively.

The photographic coverage obtained by Benson's PR Spitfires was crucial to the planning of the attack and in its subsequent evaluation, although a true and accurate assessment of the damage could not be measured until after the

Top Left: The smashed remains of the Mohne dam power house, washed 250 yards downstream of its original position by the flood waters.

Above Left: A general view of the Mohne dam taken in 1945, the breach repaired, but with rubble at its foot to show where once the power house had stood.

Left: In the event of a torpedo attack on the dam, anti-torpedo nets were installed (left) and floats (foreground) supporting timber deflectors as a last defence.

Right: Located six miles southwest of the Mohne, the Sorpe dam contained 26,208 million US gallons of water and had a different construction to the Mohne dam that made it a more difficult structure to breach. In the event, it withstood attacks by two Lancasters and remained intact.

SORPE DAM
(After attack)
K 1559
Neg. No. 24689

war had ended. In fact, post-war evaluation by the British Bombing Survey Unit revealed that the effects of the dams raid on German industry were not as dire as had been predicted.

The dams raid marked a turning point in the wider use of intelligence photographs obtained by specialised photo-reconnaissance aircraft. Up until this point in the war such activities were kept closely guarded secrets from the press and the public at large. But when national newspapers carried photographs of the breached Mohne dam on their front pages the day after the attack, provided by the Air Ministry, the selective use of such material as effective propaganda soon became clear to the British government.

No 617 SQUADRON AIRCRAFT and CREWS

Primary Force
1. Wg Cdr G. P. Gibson ED932-G (Squadron Commander)
2. Flt Lt J. V. Hopgood ED925-M*
3. Flt Lt H. B. Martin ED909-P
4. Sqn Ldr H. M. Young ED887-A*
5. Flt Lt D. J. H. Maltby ED906-J
6. Flt Lt D. J. Shannon ED929-L
7. Sqn Ldr H. E. Maudslay ED937-Z*
8. Flt Lt W. Astell ED864-B*
9. Plt Off L. G. Knight ED912-N

Secondary Force
1. Flt Lt J. C. McCarthy ED825-T
2. Flt Lt R. N. G. Barlow ED927-E*
3. Flt Lt J. L. Munro ED921-W†
4. Plt Off V. W. Byers ED934-K*
5. Plt Off G. Rice ED936-H†

Mobile Reserve Force
1. Plt Off W. H. T. Ottley ED910-C*
2. Plt Off L. J. Burpee ED865-S*
3. Flt Sgt K. W. Brown ED918-F
4. Flt Sgt W. C. Townsend ED886-O
5. Flt Sgt C. T. Anderson ED914-Y

*denotes missing in action
†denotes abortive sortie

Above Right: The Eder dam held back 73,528 million US gallons of water and suffered the same catastrophic fate as its smaller cousin, the Mohne.

Right: Thirty miles downstream of the Eder, parts of the industrial city of Kassel remained flooded a month after the raid.

Above: In this post-war general view of the Eder dam, it can be seen that the emergency sluices destroyed in the attack by No 617 Squadron, were not reconstructed.

Left: Another post-war view of the Eder dam, showing the temporary parapet.

OPERATION "GOMORRAH"

3 THE BOMBING OF HAMBURG —JULY-AUGUST 1943

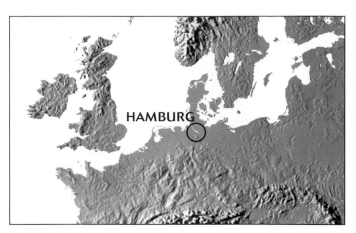

MISSION AIM

To dislocate general city life in Hamburg through area bombing, leading to the disruption of industrial production in the city's famous shipyards, and the undermining of civilian morale to the point where it would collapse.

BACKGROUND

The importance of the North Sea port of Hamburg, the second largest city in Germany and home to more than 1.5 million people during World War II, was well known to British planners at the Air Ministry. It had been bombed by Bomber Command 98 times before since the outbreak of war, but now they were certain that a sustained aerial bombardment of the city would lead to its complete physical destruction, with serious implications for the Reich's industrial output and the morale of the German people. They estimated it would take at least 10,000 tons of bombs to do the job, dropped over a period of several days. Since the spring of 1941, the RAF's heavy bomber force had been going through a progressive re-equipment programme. Soon most of its squadrons would be equipped with the new generation of four-engined heavy bombers capable of carrying bigger bomb loads and further than their twin-engined predecessors.

On May 27, 1943, RAF Bomber Command Headquarters issued Operations Order No 173 to all operational heavy bomber groups in which plans were outlined for the destruction of Hamburg using all of the RAF's available heavy

bomber squadrons. A series of maximum effort raids were to be flown by night and augmented during daylight with further attacks by heavy bomber aircraft of the US 8th Air Force. The raids were significant in that they marked the beginning of the Combined Bomber Offensive and the phenomenon of what later became known as "round-the-clock" bombing.

The series of attacks was to be mounted by eight squadrons of Lancasters and Wellingtons from No 1 Group, which was then in process of converting from its aging Wellingtons to become an all-Lancaster group; nine squadrons from No 3 Group, comprising mainly Stirlings, but with one squadron of Lancaster Mk IIs (No 115) and another of Wellingtons, Mosquitoes, and Halifaxes (No 192); seven squadrons of Halifaxes and one of Wellingtons from No 4 Group; ten squadrons of Lancasters from No 5 Group; and four squadrons of Halifaxes and

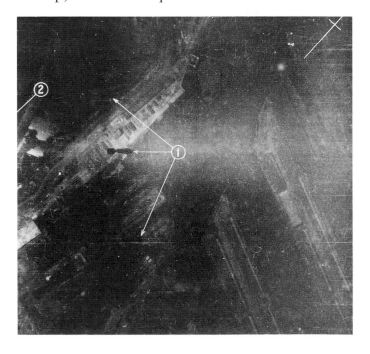

Right: Hamburg was an important German seaport in World War II and had been visited by RAF Bomber Command on many occasions before Operation "Gomorrah" in summer 1943. This aiming point photograph was taken on the night on November 30/December 1, 1941, by one of the 181 bombers that raided the city, and shows a stick of bombs falling towards the docks.

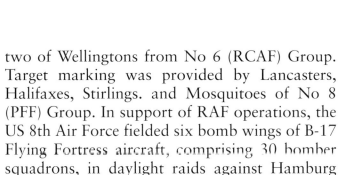

Left: These three photographs show how photo-reconnaissance located and the monitored the development of a new naval base and U-boat pens on the Rusch canal at Hamburg over a period of nine months from June 1941 to March 1942. The city's prominent dock basins showed up well on the H2S radar screens of RAF bombers during Operation "Gomorrah."

two of Wellingtons from No 6 (RCAF) Group. Target marking was provided by Lancasters, Halifaxes, Stirlings. and Mosquitoes of No 8 (PFF) Group. In support of RAF operations, the US 8th Air Force fielded six bomb wings of B-17 Flying Fortress aircraft, comprising 30 bomber squadrons, in daylight raids against Hamburg on two consecutive days.

Hamburg was an important choice as a target for several tactical reasons. Although it was beyond "Oboe" range, with its prominent situation at the wide mouth of the river Elbe and its massive dock basins, it was easily recognizable from the air on the bomber navigators' H2S radar screens, thereby helping accurate navigation and bombing. Because Hamburg was covered by no fewer than 15 radar-equipped defense boxes and nine fighter stations in the Kammhuber Line, the employment of a new and top secret countermeasures device from the Allied inventory was to be used for the first time operationally. It was hoped the device, code-named "Window," would paralyze the German radar defense network when great clouds of metallized paper strips were dropped from the attacking bombers on their approach to the enemy coast, swamping their radar screens with spurious returns. In theory, the enemy defenses would have been blinded.

The RAF's area offensive gained momentum during the summer of 1943 with ever greater numbers of heavy bombers pulverizing the German heartland in the battle of the Ruhr between March and early July, and then Hamburg beginning in late July. Damage to German cities was becoming so extensive that the photographic interpreters at CIU Medmenham had to invent new methods whereby the level of damage could be assessed. Prior to this date, interpreters would report on damage incidents on a street-by-street basis, but now that area bombing had begun in earnest and the fire raids on Hamburg were about to lay waste a whole city, this method became pointless and impracticable. But when the PR pictures of

Hamburg arrived at Medmenham at the end of July 1943 it seemed more a case of measuring damage by the square mile. The picture mosaic built up from dozens of photographic prints was so vast that it covered a whole large table.

As in any other operation flown by Bomber Command, each group headquarters created a picture of the night's work based on individual aircrew debriefing reports and aiming point photographs. In turn they sent copies of their conclusions to Bomber Command HQ and to the Operational Research Section, but this whole narrative was quickly confirmed or refuted by the PRU photos taken on the following day.

THE COURSE OF THE BATTLE

The first raid on the city of Hamburg came on the night of July 24/25, 1943, when a powerful force of 791 RAF heavy bombers, comprising 354 Lancasters, 239 Halifaxes, 120 Stirlings, and 68 Wellingtons, began taking-off from airfields in England at about 22.00hrs. Heading out across the North Sea, bundles of "Window" were discharged from each aircraft as it approached Hamburg and as predicted the German radar defenses quickly fell into disarray. Aircraft of the Pathfinder Force began by marking the target using H2S at 01.00hrs, and the first of 2,396 tons of bombs began to fall from the Main Force aircraft five minutes later. The

whole raid was over before 02.00hrs on July 25, and Hamburg had been dealt the first of a series of heavy punches. Bomber Command had lost only 12 bombers, thanks to the effect of "Window" on the German defenses.

Shortly after lunch on the 25th, 123 aircraft of the US 8th Air Force's 1st Bombardment Wing comprising the 91st, 303rd, 351st, 379th, 381st, and 384th Bomb Groups, took-off to bomb the Blohm & Voss U-boat yard and the Klockner aero-engine factory at Hamburg. Both primary targets were badly affected by smoke from the RAF's bombing of the previous night and American losses amounted to 15 B-17 Fortresses shot down by German defenses.

C.I.U. Damage Plot
HAMBURG Nº2

RAF plans to raid Hamburg again on the night of July 25/26, were abandoned after the pilot of a 1409 Met Flight Mosquito flying from RAF Wyton in Cambridgeshire reported that smoke was still obscuring the target. Instead, Harris switched the attention of his bombers to the Ruhr city of Essen for the night.

At 09.00hrs on the morning of the 26th, 121 aircraft from the same American Bombardment Wing took-off once more for Hamburg where they were to bomb the same targets as the previous day, the U-boat yard and the aero-engine factory. Despite a high number of abortive sorties, the American force succeeded in causing damage to many industrial premises, for the loss of just two B-17 Fortresses. The most important result of this raid was a direct hit on one of the two main electricity generating stations in the city, putting it out of action for a month.

For the citizens of Hamburg, late July had been far hotter than expected and they found themselves sweltering in a freak heatwave. The weather on Tuesday, July 27, was even hotter than on the preceding days. That night, Harris ordered 727 heavy bombers to attack the city using much the same tactics as on the raid of the 24th/25th. For operational reasons, the proportion of incendiary to high explosive in the bomb loads of the Halifaxes and Stirlings was increased on this occasion, a decision that was to wreak even further and unexpected destruction than before. The combination of a particularly

Above and Above Left: Post-raid damage assessment photographs of Hamburg by CIU Medmenham show thousands of acres of relatively built-up area completely devastated after the firestorm. By the war's end, 75 percent of the city's built-up area had been destroyed by Allied bombing.

Below: Smoke from the combined effects of the RAF's heavy night raid of July 24/25 and the USAAF's daylight attack on the 25th, obscures the area north of the docks, under attack here during the USAAF's second daylight raid, on the 26th. The Neuhof power station (bottom right) was seriously damaged in this raid.

SA 417
HAMBURG
26:7:43
Annotated Print Nº I
Neg. Nº 27634

high air temperature caused by the heatwave, a low humidity due to lack of rainfall, and concentrated bombing, caused a large number of fires to take hold in the densely built-up working class districts of the city. Soon the fires joined together into one huge conflagration, sucking in all available oxygen with the force of a storm. The result was a phenomenon that became known as "firestorm," and it raged out of control for some three hours and only subsided when all combustible material had been consumed. The RAF had dropped more than 2,300 tons of bombs for the loss of 17 aircraft, but Hamburg was in a state of panic. About 40,000 of its inhabitants had been killed in the firestorm, most by suffocation when the air was drawn out of their basement shelters. In the days immediately following this raid, 1.2 million people fled the city to seek sanctuary in the surrounding countryside and further afield.

During the period of the RAF's four night raids, long-range Spitfire PR XIs of No 541 and 542 Squadrons from Benson made five photo-reconnaissance runs over the city without loss. It was one such sortie on the morning of July 29 that returned with evidence showing weather over the city was clear, and the thick smoke that continued to billow up from the areas blighted by the firestorm was being carried well clear of the city by the wind.

With this recce report in mind, Harris ordered the third RAF night attack on Hamburg on the 29th/30th, when 777 aircraft raided the still-burning city. Target marking by the Pathfinders was again by H2S and very heavy bombing caused widespread fire to take hold, something the hard-pressed city fire brigade could do little to control, although this time—mercifully—no firestorm developed. By now, the city's radar defenses had recovered from their initial disability and fighters and flak claimed 28 of the attacking force.

The fourth and final raid in this devastating series of attacks was carried out on the night of August 2/3, by 740 aircraft comprising 329 Lancasters, 235 Halifaxes, 105 Stirlings, 66 Wellingtons, and 5 Mosquitoes. However, the raid soon turned into a disaster for the RAF when a large thunderstorm over Germany produced towering cloud formations that reached up to a height of 20,000ft, causing many of the Halifaxes, Wellingtons, and Stirlings to turn back early or bomb alternative targets because

Below and Below Right: An aiming point photograph and subsequent bomb plot of the Hamburg docks area, compiled from photographs taken by individual aircraft of the USAAF's 1st Bombardment Wing following its daylight attack on the afternoon of July 25, 1943.

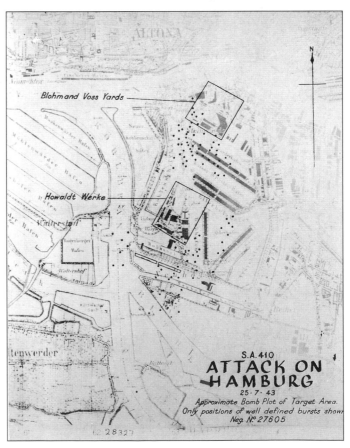

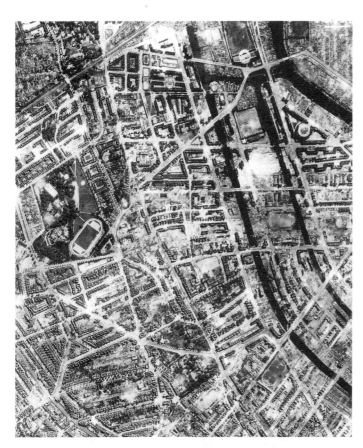

Above Left and Above: Spitfire PR XIs of Nos 541 and 542 Squadrons made five recce runs over Hamburg during the period of the RAF's four "Gomorrah" raids. The devastation caused by the firestorm is plain to see in these pictures.

Left: Piecemeal destruction of the working class neighborhood of Hammerbeck (top right) close to the dock area is evident following the third raid on July 29/30. Miraculously, some buildings remain apparently unscathed, although reconnaissance from ground level could prove otherwise.

of their inferior height performance. Of the 30 aircraft that were lost, some were undoubtedly due to the dreadful weather conditions but most fell to flak and fighters. The attack was therefore left to the Lancasters of the force, of which 13 failed to return. Although regarded as a wasted trip by many crews who flew on this final raid against Hamburg, a total of 1,426 tons of bombs was dropped on the reeling city, making a total of 8,621 tons that had been delivered by the RAF in the four raids.

Above Left and Left: These two photographs were taken secretly by an Allied agent in Hamburg after the firestorm and reveal the apocalyptic aftermath of the inferno that killed some 40,000 inhabitants of the city.

Right: Three oil refineries in Hamburg/Harburg burn after a daylight attack by more than 500 B-17 aircraft on June 20, 1944, captured on camera by a high-flying USAAF F-5 Lightning PR aircraft.

Below: Hamburg continued to receive the regular attention of Allied bombers long after many areas of the city had been reduced to rubble in the "Gomorrah" attacks. Heavy daylight raids against Hamburg's oil refineries by B-17 and B-24 aircraft of the USAAF caused substantial damage, photographed here on June 19, 1944, by an aircraft of the USAAF's 14th PR Squadron flying from Mount Farm.

PERFORMANCE

The Hamburg raids of July-August 1943 demonstrated the devastating effects of sustained area bombing and they came close to causing panic among the Nazi hierarchy. Speaking after the war, Reich Armaments Minister Albert Speer stated that the effects of these raids could only be compared to a major earthquake and that further heavy attacks against six more German cities would have brought Germany to its knees. But Bomber Harris failed to grasp this opportunity, loathe to risk his crews returning time and again to the same targets.

Over a period of 10 days a total of 3,091 sorties had been flown by the RAF for the loss of 87 aircraft. In excess of 6,000 acres of the city had been reduced to smouldering rubble while more than 41,000 of its inhabitants had been killed and 37,000 seriously injured. When the firestorm was at its height on July 27/28, its fiery mantle covered an area of 5,400 acres in which air temperatures soared to 1,800°F and gale-force winds gusted up to 150mph ripping open buildings and tearing up trees.

The raids were also significant for a number of other reasons: they marked the first occasion in World War II that the USAAF's heavy bombers had been invited to join in a Bomber Command operation; the first time that radar countermeasures had been deployed by Bomber Command to influence the outcome of a raid; and for the CIU at Medmenham it marked the turning point in its methods of assessing bomb damage to German cities subjected to area attack.

Above Right and Right: Later in the war, precision bombing by specially modified Lancaster of the RAF's No 617 Squadron inflicted further damage on the dock area with 12,000lb "Tallboy" deep-penetration bombs. Their targets were the U-boat pens at Hamburg-Finkenwarder indicate bomb strikes.

Far Right, Top: This post-war oblique photograph reveals extensive damage in the Hamburg dock area.

Far Right, Bottom: German U-boat construction continued in the shipyards of Hamburg despite the obvious chaos caused by Allied bombing to the docks and to shipyard workers' homes in the city.

RAF BOMBER COMMAND

Front-line squadrons, July-August 1943

No 1 Group, HQ: Bawtry Hall, Yorks
12 Sqn Lancaster I, III
100 Sqn Lancaster I, III
101 Sqn Lancaster I, III
103 Sqn Lancaster I, III
166 Sqn Wellington III, X
300 Sqn Wellington III
305 Sqn Wellington IV
460 Sqn Lancaster I, III

No 3 Group, HQ: Exning, Suffolk
15 Sqn Stirling I, III
75 Sqn Stirling I
90 Sqn Stirling I
115 Sqn Lancaster II
149 Sqn Stirling I, III
192 Sqn Wellington, Mosquito, Halifax
214 Sqn Stirling I, III
218 Sqn Stirling I, III
620 Sqn Stirling

No 4 Group, HQ: Heslington Hall, Yorks
10 Sqn Halifax II
51 Sqn Halifax II
76 Sqn Halifax II/V
77 Sqn Halifax II
78 Sqn Halifax II
102 Sqn Halifax II
158 Sqn Halifax II
466 Sqn Wellington X

No 5 Group, HQ: St Vincent's, Grantham, Lincs
9 Sqn Lancaster I, III
44 Sqn Lancaster I, III
49 Sqn Lancaster I, III
50 Sqn Lancaster I, III
57 Sqn Lancaster I, III
61 Sqn Lancaster I, III
106 Sqn Lancaster I, III
207 Sqn Lancaster I, III
467 Sqn Lancaster I, III
619 Sqn Lancaster I, III

No 6 (RCAF) Group, HQ: Allerton Park, Yorks
408 Sqn Halifax II
419 Sqn Halifax II
427 Sqn Halifax II
428 Sqn Halifax II
429 Sqn Wellington
432 Sqn Wellington

No 8 (PFF) Group, HQ: Wyton, Hunts
7 Sqn Lancaster I, III, Stirling I, III
35 Sqn Halifax II
83 Sqn Lancaster I, III
97 Sqn Lancaster I, III
156 Sqn Lancaster I, III
405 Sqn Halifax
139 Sqn Mosquito

1409 Met Flt Mosquito

US 8th AIR FORCE

VIIIth Bomber Command, front-line squadrons, July 1943

1st Bomb Wing, HQ: Brampton Grange
91st Bomb Group
(322nd, 323rd, 324th, 401st BS) B-17
303rd Bomb Group
(358th, 359th, 360th, 427th BS) B-17
351st Bomb Group
(408th, 409th, 410th, 411th BS) B-17
379th Bomb Group
(524th, 525th, 526th, 527th BS) B-17
381st Bomb Group
(532nd, 533rd, 534th, 535th BS) B-17
384th Bomb Group
(544th, 545th, 546th, 547th BS) B-17

Above Right and Right: On July 25, 1943, as B-17s of the 8th Air Force's 1st Bomber Wing were pounding Hamburg, 141 Fortresses of the 4th Bomber Wing were despatched to Kiel. Four of its aircraft went missing including one from the 94th Bomb Group that ditched. These photographs show the ditched aircraft being dropped a lifeboat. The crew would be recovered safely. Fifteen of 1st Bomber Wing's B-17s did not return home from Hamburg.

OPERATION "CERBERUS"

4 THE CHANNEL DASH BY *SCHARNHORST & GNEISENAU,* FEBRUARY 12, 1942

MISSION AIM

To identify, track, and locate the German Kriegsmarine's major capital ships and facilitate their destruction

BACKGROUND

In the early days of World War II it was not such a difficult task to keep watch on the German capital ships, for those not actually at sea in September 1939 were in German ports and those ports were only in northern Germany. They were all in one general area, and to get to the open sea, they had to navigate between Norway and Scotland. They could, of course, head southwest to the English Channel but that was hardly an option open to them.

However, once France fell the French Atlantic ports around Brest were opened up; if any big ships did break out of their north German confines, they could always head across the Bay of Biscay to the sanctuary of these peninsula harbors.

The other area of interest, of course, was the Mediterranean. Once Italy came into the war on the Axis side in June 1940, British forces in the Mediterranean were up against Mussolini's big ships. Added to this, after the French collapse a large part of the French Navy, now under Vichy's control, was harbored at ports along the Moroccan coast, at such places as Casablanca, Oran, Rabat, and Port Layautey. No sooner had the French surrendered than any navy ships in British or allied ports were seized, but not those in Morocco. At Oran and Mers-el-Kebir were the *Dunkerque* and the *Strasbourg,* modern battlecruisers built to be superior to the German battlecruisers *Scharnhorst* and *Gneisenau.* Failure to surrender these and other French ships to the British led to the attack on them by Royal Navy airmen on July 3, 1940. Several ships were

sunk or damaged although the *Strasbourg* escaped to Toulon.

The British were already well aware of the dangers posed by such large ships. In the early days of the war the pocket-battleship *Admiral Graf Spee* had slipped out of Germany and sunk several ships in the Atlantic before being damaged and forced into Montevideo, outside which, finding escape impossible, she was scuttled on December 18, 1939. During the Norwegian campaign the *Scharnhorst* had sunk the carrier HMS *Glorious* with large loss of life, and then the mighty *Bismarck* had sortied out on a mission that ended in her destruction—but not before she had sent the pride of the Royal Navy, HMS *Hood,* to the bottom with all but a handful of survivors. Little wonder that the British High Command needed to keep a close eye on these ships.

THE COURSE OF THE BATTLE

The best way of keeping tabs on them was by photo-reconnaissance. This would show, in the main, two things: first, that they were where they were supposed to be; and second, close inspection of the aerial photographs would hopefully indicate if a ship was being supplied with materials consistent with a sailing. The Royal Navy always had submarines lurking in the North Sea just in case a battleship should make a sudden run for the open sea, especially in times of bad weather when the regular air reconnaissance either could not fly, or the weather over the harbors proved too poor to make a photo run.

The PR pilots were briefed daily upon what they were looking for and they took great care in their navigation. They were expected to fly for several hours over enemy territory, much of it over Germany itself, and needed to know where they were at all times. This would be important, for often fuel would be a critical factor if they encountered adverse winds, or took too long to pinpoint their position if they did lose their way. It is an odd thing that their best protection, other than speed in their eventual stripped down, unarmed aircraft, was cloud—yet it was cloud that would cause the worst problems over a target area. To operate their cameras successfully needed height, as well as a straight run, generally above 26,000ft and often as high as 30-31,000ft. Over Europe, cloud is always a feature.

When the *Scharnhorst*, *Gneisenau*, and the cruiser *Prinz Eugen* finally did get out and then went into Brest, photo-reconnaissance was essential, again in keeping watch on these ships, for if they were allowed to get back into the Atlantic, their destructive potential would be disastrous for Allied ship convoys, escorted usually at most by destroyers. By reading through the reports of No 1 PRU we can see how seriously this observation on the German battleships and battlecruisers became. No 1 PRU operated Spitfires from RAF Benson, in Oxfordshire, in the main, but also used the Coastal Command airfield at St Eval in Cornwall to watch Brest, and also Wick in Scotland to cover some of the northern Germany ports and Norway.

As an example of the range of these Spitfires, on January 19, 1941, Flt Lt P. Corbishley, DFC, took-off from Benson at 10.30hrs to photograph the Italian ports of Genoa and Spezia, the latter being where German and Italian submarines were based. In this instance bad weather prevented him from completing his task and he eventually made landfall at Corsica before continuing on to the island of Malta, landing at 15.45hrs—a flight of 5hr 15min.

At 11.15hrs on March 4, 1941, Flt Lt K. F. Arnold headed out from St Eval in bad weather to fly to Brest, but over the target area the sun was shining. Despite heavy flak he observed a "Hipper" class cruiser in the docks. Although later PR Spitfires were famed for being unarmed, the early Spitfires did carry weapons, and on this occasion, Arnold found himself near Guipavas airfield and spotted a Messerschmitt Bf109 fighter taking-off in his direction. Arnold dived on the Messerschmitt, firing from 800yd and it went straight into the ground. He then flew over the aerodrome shooting up parked aircraft and running personnel from 200ft.

Suspecting the *Scharnhorst* and *Gneisenau* were in Brest, it needed not only confirmation but a constant watch and during periods of adverse weather the Royal Navy became very twitchy if reports were not received regularly. On March 28, 1941, following five days of bad

Above: High level photograph of Brest taken on March 28, showing the locations of *Scharnhorst* and *Gneisenau* and their anti-torpedo booms.

Below: Night photograph of Brest taken during a bombing attack by No 115 Squadron on May 7, 1941. (Note the photo-flash has produced a reflection indicated 7.) The interpreters have identified *Scharnhorst* and *Gneisenau* (1), bomb bursts (2 and 3), a flare (4), and a gunflash (5).

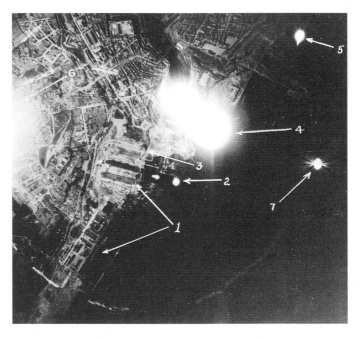

weather and anxious to know if they were indeed there—and staying there—Benson and St Eval pilots were being urged to make a trip. Finally Plt Off Green took-off from St Eval at 15.15hrs and flew through atrocious weather, rain, and zero visibility until he finally broke cloud 60 miles from the English coast. Arriving over Brest he found it covered with cloud so he cruised around Douarenez Bay, trying to make a visual recce through gaps. With nothing of importance seen after 20 minutes, he finally selected a gap over Brest itself and made two quick photo runs over the docks from 22,000ft, despite considerable AA fire. His film revealed and established that the two battlecruisers were indeed there.

Following Arnold's strafe on March 4, Flt Lt A. L. Taylor, DFC, whilst on a PR sortie to Le Bourget airfield near Paris and then Dieppe harbor, saw aircraft on the ground at the former and strafed several Heinkel He111 bombers he spotted on the west side of the base. Aggression was all very well, but it could endanger valuable film. This, added to the need for speed and lightness, later led to gun-less Spitfires. Alistair Lennox Taylor, of course, was one of the PR greats. An RAF pilot since 1936 he had served in France on Battles before going to PRU and in 1940-41 was to receive the DFC and two bars.

There was another attempt at Genoa and Spezia on April 14, this time flown by Sgt W. Morgan. Such was the weather that Bill Morgan had to fly—and navigate—blind all the way to Genoa, although he did spot the Alps once, and then fly blind all the way back. Because of head winds and drifts he lost his way and was about to bale out as his fuel became exhausted, but at that moment he saw the White Cliffs of Dover and managed a landing in a pole-studded field (anti-invasion obstacles) without damage to Spitfire or film, and with just two gallons of petrol remaining. He had been in the air for 7hr 10min.

Alistair Taylor flew to Kiel and Cuxhaven on June 17, taking photos from 30,000ft. Since the last recce five days earlier, the *Tirpitz* and *Lützow* had arrived in Kiel as his film showed. Also there was the pocket-battleship *Admiral Scheer*, and the 8in cruiser *Admiral Hipper*. His

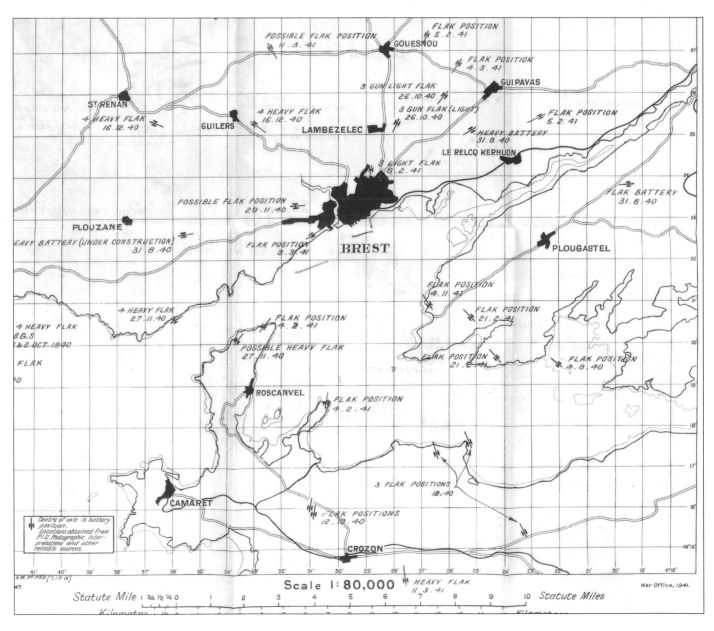

ALLIED PHOTO RECONNAISSANCE

film also revealed that, for the first time, attempts were being made to camouflage these major naval units.

Flg Off D. W. Steventon went to Kiel in adverse weather on August 6. There was considerable anxiety regarding the location of the *Tirpitz* and as a result the sortie had to be flown. On his return flight, having flown through large storm clouds above which he could not climb, his aircraft became completely iced-up, affecting controls, instruments, and cockpit canopy. After losing control and going into an inverted spin he finally regained control at 7,000ft and got home. However, his Spitfire had to be returned to the makers as both wings were wrinkled and the fuselage buckled. The film, once developed, clearly showed the location of the battleship, so their Lordships—and no doubt Steventon—breathed a sigh of relief.

All this shows just how important the Admiralty and the RAF thought it was to keep on top of the big ships' locations. On September 2, Plt Off Busbridge made a tour of Hamburg, Bremerhaven, Wilhelmshaven, Bremen, Amsterdam, and Vegasak, photos being taken of the 8in cruiser *Seydlitz*, thus confirming its continued presence in Werfthaven, Bremen. As can be imagined, navigating and flying a single-engined fighter over such distances, as well as watching out for hostile fighters, needed a very special type of pilot.

Two days later two pilots went north again: Flg Off N. J. Bonner to Copenhagen, confirmed by film that the *Leipzig* had left harbor. Flg Off Whitehead went to Kiel and the Kiel Canal, making photo runs from 28,000ft. These revealed the *Tirpitz* at the entrance to the inner dockyard basin, the *Leipzig* still where she should be, but that the *Admiral Scheer* had left, with the *Admiral Hipper* in a dry dock.

The Germans only ever had one aircraft carrier—the *Graf Zeppelin*, which in the event never saw action, but it was something that needed to be watched—just in case. On

Left: Map of Brest showing flak battery locations as at March 28, 1941.

Above Right: No 218 Squadron bombed Brest on May 7, 1941. A photograph from one of their aircraft also shows the two battlecruisers and bomb explosions 300 yards away.

Right: Brest taken by PR aircraft on July 21, 1941: the PR mission was followed by a bombing raid three days later.

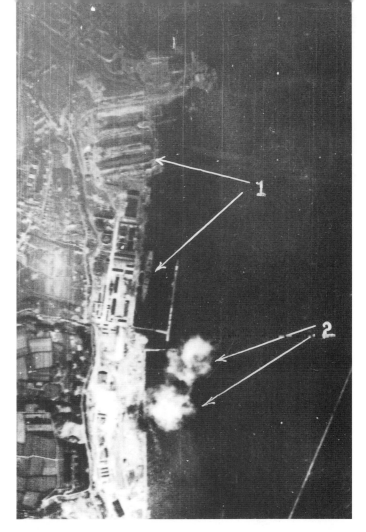

Above: Bomber Command raided Brest in daylight on December 18, 1941. Bombs can be seen falling in the right foreground, while a smokescreen is beginning to obscure the two capital ships.

September 8, 1941, Flg Off Durstan went to Stettin where she was kept. Earlier photos had shown she was far from complete but these latest ones revealed that she was nearly ready to sail.

Plt Off R. E. Walker, DFM (who would later be killed) photographed the *Admiral Scheer* on September 19 as she proceeded slowly down the river at Swindemunde off Railway Quay, but life wasn't always that easy. The next day, Flt Lt Chisholm had his engine cut out at 28,000ft over Hamburg due to tank failure. He lost 8,000ft before managing to restart it. Some days earlier Flt Sgt Fripp had had his engine cut while high over Stettin, again due to tank problems, and he lost 5,000ft before he got it sorted out. On the same day, September 4, Flg Off Bennett had covered the Biscay ports of St Nazaire, La Pallice, La Rochelle, Lorient, and Brest from St Eval. He had been attacked by three 109s over Brest and his Spitfire had been badly damaged by cannon hits but he managed to get back and made a landing at Predannack.

Sergeant Jones brought back excellent photos of Copenhagen on October 7. These revealed that a "Schlesien" class battleship had left since being seen 10 days earlier, and was probably the one found in Kiel two days earlier. Jones was at 31,000ft, 30 miles north of Kiel when his oxygen froze up. The next thing he remembers was being at 15,000ft over Wyk Island. Flying home he crossed over the Norfolk coast in cloud and almost out of fuel put down in a field, but without damage to his film or cameras.

It was back to Kiel on the 20th for Plt Off Barker, filming from 27-29,000ft the cruiser *Leipzig*, which three days earlier had been seen at the entrance to the inner dockyard basin and was now off Heikandorf, moving northeast up the Kiel Fjord. His film also confirmed the *Admiral Hipper* at the south quay at Kiel and the light cruiser *Emden* at the mole at the Torpedo Boat Harbor. The pocket-battleship *Lützow* was still in the No 6 dry dock at Kiel.

With the French ships still a possible threat, Flg Off Durstan went to Toulon, Nice, and Marseilles in October, his photos revealing the battleship *Provence*, the battlecruiser *Strasbourg* and the ex-battleships *Concorcet* and *L'Ocean* still in Toulon as they had been when photographed on August 27. A flight on October 3 by Flg Off Sinclair, operating from Gibraltar, to Tangier, Port Layautey, and Casablanca, had shown the battleship *Jean Bart* still alongside the Quai de Laude at Casablanca.

A trip back to Kiel and Hamburg by Flg Off W. J. G. Morgan on October 24 confirmed the *Admiral Scheer* had moved out of the Floating Dock No 5 at the Blohm and Voss Yard in Hamburg, where it was last seen on the 5th. There must have been a ripple of excitement on November 15, the film from Plt Off A. M. D. Gunn's Spitfire showing that the aircraft carrier *Graf Zeppelin* had left Stettin. However, she, like so many of Hitler's big ships, while always a threat, were rarely a problem. He seemed to protect them, hoping perhaps that one day his navy could roam the high seas in search of his enemies, but for the most part they just sat in harbors.

As 1942 began, the coverage did not let up. Flg Off J. Morgan did a tour of Stettin, Politz, Swindemunde, Rostock, and the Lübeck areas on January 6. It was thought the *Admiral Scheer* and the *Lützow* had moved from Swindemunde, and so it proved by his pictures. Four days later Flg Off Durstan found the *Lützow* in Kiel, but on her own. A rapid search located the *Admiral Scheer* the next day, Plt Off Gunn finding her five miles off Swindemunde, although he could not take photos because of the weather, but he brought back a visual report of his sighting.

Towards the end of January, the *Tirpitz* was again the focus of attention, Flt Lt Fane bringing back pictures of her on the 23rd, lying close inshore at the head of Arsfiord and protected by a torpedo boom. Flt Sgt Tomlinson again photographed her on the 29th. When in 1944 strikes were made against her, it was PR information which helped provide the planners their best way of approaching her by air.

Meantime, Spitfires from St Eval kept an ever-watchful eye on Brest and its three ugly sisters, while aircraft from Gibraltar kept Oran, Tafaroui, etc under surveillance. On January 15, 1942, Flg Off Sayce was able to confirm the *Dunkerque* was in her usual position at Mersel-Kebir with a double torpedo boom.

The PRU also flew Maryland twin-engined aircraft from Gibraltar to keep watch on the Moroccan ports. Flg Off N. D. Sinclair flew one such aircraft to Casablanca, Rabat, Port Layautey, and Erdla, taking pictures of the *Jean Bart* in her usual berth at Casablanca, and con-

Below: Map showing the passage of the *Scharnhorst*, *Gneisenau*, and *Prinz Eugen* in the Channel Dash on February 12, 1942. (This map was produced by the Admiralty in 1948.)

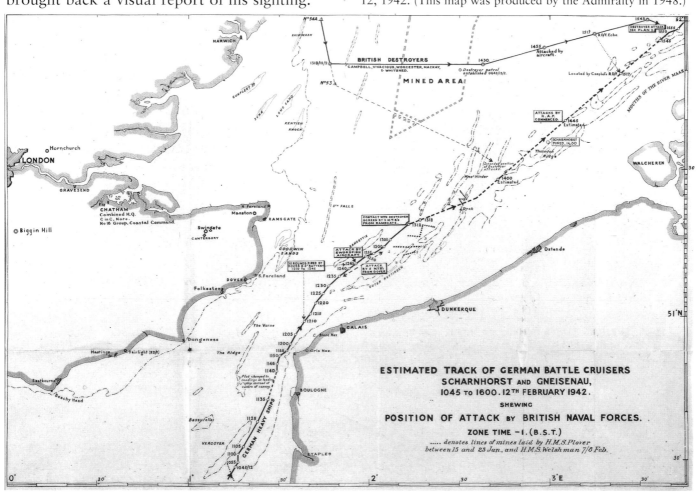

firmed a "Galissioniere" class cruiser was in port.

On February 12, 1942, the almost unthinkable happened. The *Scharnhorst*, *Gneisenau*, and *Prinz Eugen* finally left Brest and made their now famous "Dash" up the English Channel in order to make a German port without going all the way round the British Isles. It was a bold move and one that in the event, by its sheer impertinence, succeeded, much to the indignation of the Royal Navy and RAF. As in all such things, circumstances and chance gave the Germans the edge, but it must have been frustrating for the PR boys who had been watching constantly for any signs that they might try a break out.

Operation "Fuller," the plan devised to counter a move by the ships up the Channel, had been in force since the previous April, the initial thought being they might try a break through the Channel between April 30 and May 4, 1941. Perhaps some complacency had set in—for whatever reason, what happened was not one of British photo-reconnaissance highpoints during World War II. Despite intercepting German Enigma messages about the intended Channel Dash, the British were unable to stop *Scharnhorst*, *Gneisenau*, and *Prinz Eugen* sailing from Brest to Germany.

The planned movement—the Germans called it Operation "Cerberus"—had two main compo-nents: the German Navy would keep a passage close to the French coast clear of mines to allow the warships a fast, clear channel, and Oberst Adolf Galland would control a Luftwaffe air screen that would move with the warships.

The intended departure of the warships from Brest was delayed by an air raid: a lucky coincidence because it stopped them running into the submarine HMS *Sealion*, which had entered Brest Roads by the afternoon tide and was now leaving to recharge its batteries. At the same time, the patrolling RAF Hudson's radar failed and it went off station at 19.30hrs. Its replacement finished its patrol at 22.45hrs just as the warships sailed—and it would be midnight before there was aircraft surveillance of the area again. By then it was too late: the birds had flown.

All the way up the Cherbourg peninsula and on along the Normandy coast, British radar spotted unusual activity and passed it off as a number of things including an air-sea rescue operation. It was not until mid-morning that the warships were spotted, and two hours later before an attack was attempted—by No 825 Squadron, Fleet Air Arm in antiquated Swordfish torpedo aircraft; 825's CO, Lt Cdr E. Esmonde, would win a posthumous Victoria Cross for his bravery, but despite pressing home their attack, no damage was done to the German vessels until Scharnhorst struck a mine at 14.30hrs—but, despite this, soon she was steaming again at 25kts.

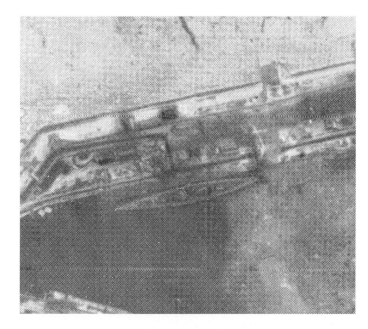

Poor visibility hampered attacks by RAF bombers and RN destroyers, and both vessels escaped. *Scharnhorst* hit another mine and just made Wilhelmshaven; *Gneisenau* also hit two mines but reached Kiel along with Prinz Eugen.

PERFORMANCE

Overall, the photo-reconnaissance missions against the German capital ships were extraordinarily successful: the British were able to keep an eye on the major units and, even if—through bad weather or technical problems—they could not do so through use of the Mark I eyeball, Enigma was able to supply much needed assistance. But despite all this, the *Kriegesmarine* had its triumphs and Operation "Cerberus" was one of them.

Above Left: Scharnhorst berthed on the south wall of the Hipper Haven at Wilhelshaven, photographed on February 22 after her successful Dash up the Channel 10 days earlier.

Left: The *Gneisenau* in Kiel, October 1942: the three arrows indicate empty gun turrets, while "A" shows where they are on the dock.

Below: PR photograph of the port of Hamburg taken on March 13, 1942, showing the 8in cruiser *Admiral Hipper* (1), which had arrived on the 2nd. The other ship (2) is an unnamed liner launched early in the war, showing no signs of further work. Behind her are three 500-ton U-boats.

Far Left and Below Left: No 1 PRU photograph taken on February 12, 1942. The big ships had departed but the Spitfire's cameras could find nothing to photograph due to cloud and smokescreens.

OPERATION "AVALANCHE"

5 THE LANDINGS AT SALERNO, SEPTEMBER 9, 1943

MISSION AIM

To invade Italy, the "soft underbelly of Europe," roll up Italian and German defences and so be able to attack the Reich from the south.

BACKGROUND

By the time the Allies were ready to mount an invasion of Italy under the codename Operation "Avalanche," photographic reconnaissance had become a vital part of the pre-planning of all major operations. RAF Mosquitoes had ranged ever further afield to cover strategic targets as Axis forces were pushed out of North Africa and one squadron—No 60 SAAF—had mapped southern Italy and photographed aerodromes and ports as far north as latitude 46°, which took in the top half of the Adriatic.

The successful conclusion of the campaigns in the Western Desert, Sardinia, and Sicily had brought the hope that the surrender of Italian forces on September 8 would mean that such an invasion would not be necessary. Hitler's avowed intention of maintaining substantial German forces in Italy to fight, independently if necessary, rendered this hope stillborn.

The decision to invade Italy was made at the Quebec Conference of the Allied Combined Chiefs of Staff in August. Winston Churchill, emphasising his strong belief in the continuing importance of a Mediterranean strategy, persuaded Roosevelt and Gen George Marshall, both of whom had reservations, that Italy could be secured with relative ease. Undeniably, the use of Italian airfields would provide the Allied air forces with the means to expand the combined bomber offensive against Germany. These

Below: US photo interpreters prepare reconnaissance material—a vital part of the pre-planning of any operation of the magnitude of the invasion of Italy.

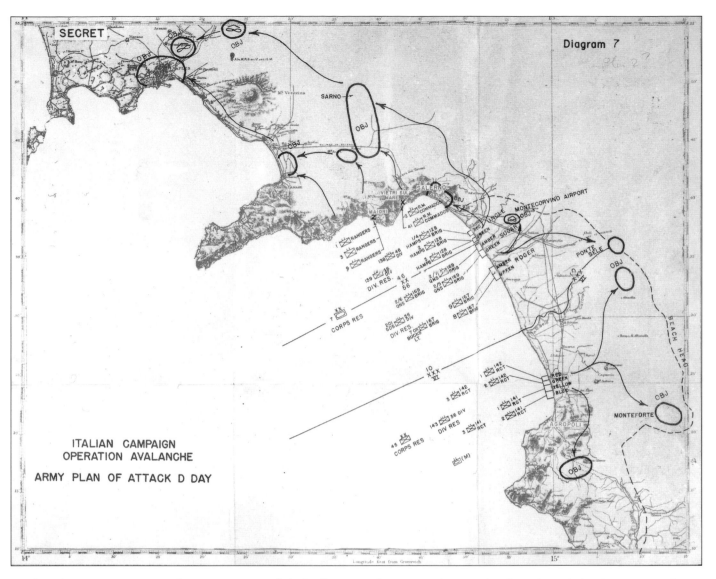

Above: Map showing the plan of attack for Operation "Avalanche" with the landing point of each Allied unit and some of the first objectives identified.

and other arguments that a successful Italian campaign would "speed the end of the war," won the day.

As a prerequisite to dual invasion thrusts by British and Canadian forces at Calabria and the US Army at Salerno, PR coverage of the Italian coastline and airfields continued as it had done for some months, Northwest African Photo Reconnaissance Wing (NWAPRW) having gradually extended the reach of its camera-equipped aircraft. By that point of the war NWAPRW represented a well-integrated Allied air organization enjoying an admirable degree of international co-operation between mainly British, US and South African personnel and units.

Relatively small numbers of aircraft were required, although the PR organization in the Mediterranean was rarely in the position of having too many examples of the right type than it could cope with, knowing that it was some way down the "pecking order" as regards the issue of new aircraft. Delays in the delivery of the right type of replacement aircraft was probably the

most irksome drawback for the operational units, as target photography of the quality that had already been achieved was not possible with simply any aircraft modified to carry cameras. The highest possible performance was mandatory if for no other reason than the Germans were quite well aware of what single high flying enemy aircraft were up to and made every effort—fortunately without too much success— to shoot them down. The PR war effort was not conducted without loss, with a number of crews and aircraft disappearing without trace. To their credit, the PR units rarely let any of their clients down: if the weather allowed a clear view of a target, sooner or later its imagery would be captured on film, often in remarkable clarity. Wartime cameras were well able to reveal minute detail from extremely high altitudes.

UNITS INVOLVED

For long-range strategic target cover, RAF units in the Mediterranean were by 1943 flying the Mosquito PR Mk IX, whose service ceiling and performance made it relatively safe from interception. Photo-reconnaissance versions of the Spitfire generally handled British tactical PR (TacPR) sorties, while the US Army Air Force, which also flew some Spitfires in this role, had for some time been relying on the F-4 and F-5.

These reconnaissance models of the P-38E and G-H Lightning had, although they lacked a second seat, the advantage of twin-engine capability and a fuselage able to accommodate a range of cameras. The Lightning was to remain the primary US PR aircraft for the duration of the war. Tactical reconnaissance work was undertaken by P-51 Mustangs and Spitfires, with older PR types such as the Maryland continuing to serve over areas in which Luftwaffe opposition was unlikely. (225 Martin Marylands due to be exported to France were diverted to Britain. Their best-known exploit was the reconnaissance leading to the attack on Taranto in November 1940.) Ex-TacPR Hurricanes were by 1943 undertaking the important role of meteorological flying in company with other second-line types.

Under the energetic command of Elliot Roosevelt, son of US President Franklin D., the entire PR organization in the Mediterranean had gradually expanded. A new Mediterranean Allied PR Wing (MAPRW) replaced the old NWAPRW, of which the USAAF element was the 3rd PRG, encompassing the 5th, 12th and 23rd Photo Squadrons, plus the 154th and the 111th PRS.

The older established RAF element also underwent change in that No 4 PRU, and what had been known as the Malta Reconnaissance Flight became, Nos 682 and 683 PR Squadrons respectively while Nos 2 and 3 PRU (which did not serve in the Mediterranean) were renumbered as Nos 680 and 681 Squadrons. No 60 Squadron, SAAF remained under RAF jurisdiction and an Armée de l'air unit, Groupe de Reconnaissance II/33 "Savoie," also equipped with PR Lightnings, was also attached to the wing. A Joint Central Interpretation Unit was also established. The increased size of the PR organization ultimately led to the adoption of USAAF wing status as the 90th PRW. This was activated in North Africa on November 22.

Below: Aerial reconnaissance photo of the Gulf of Salerno showing "Sugar" and "Roger" beaches. A cautionary note indicates that the land in front of "Roger" had covered drains and open ditches while that further inland from "Sugar" was flat and under cultivation. The Allied armies had some trouble in moving out from the beachhead.

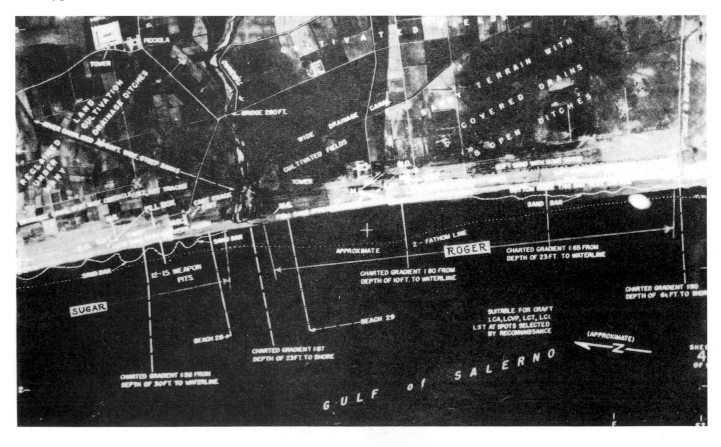

ALLIED PHOTO RECONNAISSANCE

THE COURSE OF THE BATTLE

Above: LCVPs from AKA-15 USS *Andromeda* head for Salerno, September 9, 1943.

The Italian campaign began with Operation "Baytown" on September 3, when the British Xth Corps of the Eighth Army under Lt-Gen Sir Richard McCreedy and the US VIth Corps, commanded by Maj-Gen Ernst Dawley, went ashore at Reggio di Calabria on the toe of the Italian boot. On the 9th more British forces landed on the "heel" of the country and took the port and city of Taranto. That same day Lt-Gen Mark Clark's Fifth American Army launched "Avalanche" with landings at Salerno and Paestum south of Naples.

There was considerable enemy resistance to the Salerno landings, so much so that an emergency evacuation was planned for the 13th, but by the 14th German counter-attacks were being contained, greatly aided by Allied airpower and troop reinforcements. The beachhead was all but secured although this could not prevent some German tanks only being halted within five miles of the beaches. During the night of the 17th/18th the Germans pulled back.

Close air support was increased by the securing of Paestum airfield on the 10th. From there, US fighters helped blunt regular, three times daily attacks by the Luftwaffe which mounted "hit and run" raids on the invasion fleet and beachhead. A US paratroop drop effectively prevented a dangerous German counter-attack from developing, enabling American and British troops to link up and prepare to go onto the offensive by September 20.

Throughout the rest of September the entire lower boot of Italy was captured: Naples was taken on October 1, and by the end of the following week the Allies were on the Volturno River. In the meantime US and RAF fighter, bomber, and PR units had moved to Italy in some strength, the build-up including the 111th TRS which occupied Sele. By November these and other units were supporting the Allied drive north to the point that troops were probing the defenses of the German Gustav Line.

Following the major reorganization of Allied airpower in the region which had taken place in September 1943 and which saw the formation of the 15th Air Force, the 5th PR Squadron (plus the 68th Recon Group) was allocated mainly to serve the needs of this second bomber arm. Together with the 8th in England, the 15th would provide a second force of strategic bombers to strike Germany. Its PR organization was later boosted by the 154th, the 3rd Squadron being assigned to the 12th Air Force. There was some overlap, all the PR squadrons actually contributing to the target coverage requested by the tactical and strategic air forces.

MAPRW introduced a system of air-to-ground liaison early in 1944. Prior to

Right: Overshadowed by the high ground around the Salerno beachhead which took the Allies about 10 days to clear of German troops, amphibious DUKWs shuttle to and from the LSTs. Note the balloon, rigged to ward off low flying enemy aircraft. After the Allies got bogged down on the Gustav Line, Salerno harbor would be an essential stepping-off point for Operation "Shingle," the amphibious assault on Anzio in January 1944.

Below: Landing operations in Salerno. Note the use of chicken wire to stabilize beach sand. The LCVP is from APA-90 USS *James O'Hare*, and the MP in the right-foreground has obviously heard something to make him duck.

Bottom: While the landing was unopposed, the response by the Germans was swift and brutal—the first sign that Europe's "soft underbelly" would not prove so soft. Here a bomb attack is in progress.

"Avalanche," tactical PR had had only a limited direct ground-support role due to the "localized" nature of much of the fighting in North Africa. But now that entire Allied armies were moving en masse from one sector to another over terrain with numerous natural geographical barriers, not to mention man-made obstacles, the need to provide up-to-the-minute intelligence and photo coverage in greater detail, was paramount—"Avalanche," for example, was the largest amphibious operation of the war at the time. Army officers were consequently posted to work at air headquarters and airmen undertook duty with army units, the better to foster understanding of the others' needs.

To the mass of PR coverage obtained by the specialized units was added target photos taken by combat aircraft; most medium and heavy bombers carried a strike camera to record the accuracy of raids on specific targets, the resultant prints being widely used in bomb damage assessment (BDA) and in the planning for repeat raids, which were often necessary. Tactical aircraft flying numerous armed recce sorties, contributed to the accumulated data both via the camera lens and visual observation.

If the supply of photo-reconnaissance aircraft continued to be critical at times, the training of new pilots in PR work was expanding; when it was based at San Severo in August, No 60 Squadron SAAF was placed in the awkward position of having more than enough pilots but few aircraft. More Mosquito Mk IXs were then anxiously awaited to bring the unit's complement to seven aircraft by September. On the other hand, Lt-Col James Setchell's 3rd PR Group (PG) had a surplus of aircraft and the South Africans were offered three F-5s. While they appreciated the gesture, by all accounts the pilots were not exactly impressed by the PR Lightning. Apart from missing the services of a navigator, which made life a great deal easier when flying the Mosquito, the F-5 compared unfavorably on a number of other counts. Pilots felt that it was a heavier aircraft to maneuver, particularly at the kind of altitudes—around 32-35,000ft—they adopted for the best PR results. Adverse comments were made about some of the "quaint" controls including the roll-down car-door-type cockpit panels. The Lightnings were handed back as soon as possible.

In addition to the immediate Allied objectives was the huge base complex at Foggia, which was large enough to support the greater proportion of Allied airpower committed to the battle for Italy. Foggia's dozen main and satellite airfields were secured early on September 27, enabling strategic and tactical bombers which had already waged a lengthy war of attrition against German airfields and landing grounds, to increase their pounding of targets behind the front.

As far as German air strength was concerned, months of trying in vain to achieve any headway against general Allied superiority had taken a terrible toll, particularly of fighters and ground attack aircraft. In fact, the Luftwaffe's days in Italy were numbered. At its almost fatally weak level any new build-up would have to be to the detriment of the air defense of the Reich, which Hitler would not entertain. There would be no reinforcement—instead, the air defense of the country would be handled primarily by Italian nationals who remained sympathetic to the Fascist cause by creating a new air force, the Aeronautica Nazionale Repubblicana.

By D+3 the 111th Tactical Reconnaissance Squadron (TRS), then operating under XII Air Support Command, was able to fly up to six missions per day for US Vth Corps while 225 Wing RAF undertook reconnaissance for British Xth Corps. The US unit operated P-51 Mustangs on pre-planned reconnaissance sorties and also made aircraft available on an on-call basis to spot for artillery. It was the first time that American single-seaters had helped ground gunners adjust their fire to greater effect to deal with German gun positions.

Monte Corvino airfield had opened for business "under new management" by September 8-10, having previously been selected by the Allies and largely left untouched by bombs. German artillery fire prevented its regular use for some time, however, and the securing of alternative airfields proved timely. Few problems were encountered by the PR units although most installations had been destroyed either by Allied bombing or demolition by the Germans before they evacuated.

PERFORMANCE

MAPRW now made the 3rd PRG responsible for the photography of future targets fanning out from Salerno. On January 24, 1944, Col Karl Polifka took over the wing when Roosevelt was posted back to Europe. A highly exprinced PR

Above: British 5.5-inch guns lay down a barrage on the Vitturno River Line, one of a number of fortified positions prepared by the Germans in advance of the Allied invasion of Italy.

pilot, Polifka had come to Italy via Australia and the US. He had seen considerable combat flying in the Pacific earlier in the war and could tell hair-raising stories of avoiding the attentions of Japanese "Zeroes" while on recon flights. Polifka continued to fly PR sorties in Italy.

Further honing of operational and concurrent PR activity brought a general division of responsibility in that USAAF units supported the Fifth Army on the Western coast of Italy with the RAF aligning itself with the Eighth Army on the west coast. Mosquitoes continued to range far and wide to swell the target photo files for current and future raids by Allied heavies. No 60 Squadron flew numerous tactical sorties to provide Allied field commanders with a comprehensive picture of the Italian rail and road network behind Kesselring's front line. This led to the far-reaching Operation "Strangle," the huge tactical air assault on all German transportation throughout the Italian front. It ultimately denied Kesselring the bulk of his supplies and the means to prosecute the war but this would only come after much hard fighing.

The spring of 1944 brought only marginally improved weather over Italy and the potential German and Austrian targets. All these were photographed whenever the conditions allowed and the sortie rate spiraled. But at the front, German resistance, adverse weather, and the difficult terrain all conspired to render progress up through Italy, Churchill's "soft underbelly of Europe" anything but easy. The going was often painfully slow, and casualties mounted as Kesselring's bitter defense stiffened. He was obliged to give ground but virtually every mile had to be fought for and by May the Allied timetable had slipped. As the date for the invasion of Western Europe loomed, Rome had not fallen and a sizable army was tied down on a front that had already been regarded as secondary to the main Allied thrust, which the Quebec conference had confirmed would be through Normandy.

One of the most critical items of equipment for the "Overlord" build-up was landing craft; more of them might have been used for amphibious landings in Italy to speed up Allied progress but there were simply too few to go around. The landing craft stayed in Britain and some of the troops, notably men of the British 7th Armoured and the US 82nd Airborne Division, who had so recently landed in southern Italy, returned to England in November 1943 to prepare for "Overlord." Other divisions were then sent to Italy.

In an effort to break the stalemate on the Gustav Line the Allies conceived a plan that involved an attack through Cassino and and amphibious assault on Anzio, just south of Rome. To see how this operation—"Shingle"— fared we must move to the next chapter..

The immediate result of Salerno was stalemate but, despite this, the troops could take comfort from the fact that Axis airpower was on the wane in Italy. The further north the advance moved, the greater the preponderance of friendly aircraft over the battlefield. Everything from heavy bombers to fighters sortied to assist the ground forces, to blast the factories turning out new tanks and guns, to attack supply lines miles behind the German lines thus denying them their vital supplies and to give them no peace on the battlefields. All this effort was made possible by continual aerial surveillance of German activity so that the carefully marshalled men and weaponry necessary for any counter-attack, any new thrust was soon identified. Although PR could not dictate the outcome of a battle, friendly troops were rarely caught off balance for long, their headquarters invariably being "forewarned and forearmed" with the minimum delay.

Below: After the capture of Naples, the Allies pushed upwards into Italy but became bogged down at the Vitturno River. After that the next obstacle was the River Garagliano and Monte Cassino. At Triflisco, US engineers on the south bank threw across a temporary bridge for troops and vehicles.

MONTE CASSINO

6 BREAKING THE GUSTAV LINE

MISSION AIM

For US and British forces to break through the Gustav Line and out of the Anzio bridgehead, combine forces and so open the road to Rome.

BACKGROUND

Despite fending off repeated German counter-attacks with massive air, sea, and ground bombardment, the threatened beachhead at Anzio came very near to being lost to the Allies as the enemy reacted savagely to the surprise invasion of January 22. Having previously landed at Salerno and taken heavy casualties, Lt-Gen Mark Clark's Fifth Army had by early January fought its way up the west coast of Italy and had tried but failed to work around Cassino and isolate it. A direct assault on the steep slopes appeared to be the only alternative.

In the meantime a month's bitter fighting at Anzio had succeeded in consolidating the beachhead, which was deemed more or less secure by February 20. But everyone involved in the operation knew full well a breakout had to be made soon. Equally, it was clear that this would only be possible if US and British forces could break out at Anzio and combine their considerable strength for a decisive blow against the Gustav Line. Having pulled back and fortified this front line, making maximum use of the rugged terrain, the Germans could afford to sit out Allied attempts to force a breach in it. They had to do so to open the road to Rome. But this entailed capturing Monte Cassino, situated midway beteen Naples and the Eternal City. It was a daunting prospect.

Considerable optimism nevertheless attended the opening of this campaign within a campaign

when French troops captured the mountainous area of Santa Croce. British and US forces were poised to reinforce and exploit this gain and on January 16 Allied intelligence announced its belief that the Germans would not put up great resistance to a renewed Allied drive due to "casualties, exhaustion and lack of morale." This last was qualified—but in reality all these factors were little more than wishful thinking. A closer study of recent reconnaissance photos and POW interrogation reports would have given a far more realistic impression of the hardened German troops defending much of the Gustav Line which included the town and monastery located on the heights above Cassino. Worst of

Right: A map showing Allied positions in Italy prior to the Anzio landings and army dispositions at the first attempt to bypass the Cassino defences.

all, the reports appeared to play down the superb natural defenses of the mountains and hills occupied by the Germans. who had had ample time to position tanks, SP guns, and field artillery to repel the invaders. It was this over optimism that led to the failure of the first attempt to secure Cassino.

UNITS INVOLVED

Photo coverage of those areas of the Italian front that were proving most difficult for the ground forces to penetrate was undertaken by a number of units including No 683 Squadron RAF. Having become an all-Spitfire squadron the previous June, No 683 flew two sorties a day on the Fifth Army front from mid-October, using Monte Corvino as its base. This work continued with further coverage of targets in northwestern Italy during 1944.

Aircraft attrition took its toll in all war theaters as the 111th TRS was to find. Having been issued with P-51 and P-51A model Mustangs, the 111th along with the 154th TRS had begun operations with the new type in March 1943. By the following year the supply of Allison-engined Mustangs had begun to dwindle and as other units, including the 154th, had also operated other aircraft types in the armed PR role, it

seemed prudent to group all the remaining early model Mustangs in the 111th. The squadron flew numerous armed recce missions which had the dual advantage of providing Allied intelligence with both photographic evidence and verbal situation reports by pilots—who were in a position to attack targets while engaged on their high speed, low level photo runs.

Pilots of the 90th PRW carried out test photo runs at varying altitudes from 1,500ft down to 100ft and found that an ideal average height was 300ft. This was low enough for clear pictures to be obtained by the F-5 as it gave ample lens coverage and pilot orientation. At that altitude the aircraft could also avoid all but the lightest flak and small-arms fire and allowed pilots to drop a little lower with safety if they were attacked, or to get "under the radar" when necessary. And it was often the case, with the cameras rolling at low altitude, numerous interesting installations, road and rail traffic, and other potential targets were captured on film. These "targets of opportunity" would be attacked as soon as possible after the prints were processed and distributed to combat units.

Below: The massive task of unloading supplies could hardly be hidden from the Germans, who shelled and bombed the Anzio anchorage for much of the time the Allies remained there. DUKWs ran the gauntlet of enemy shelling to complete their vital shuttle service from the ships offshore.

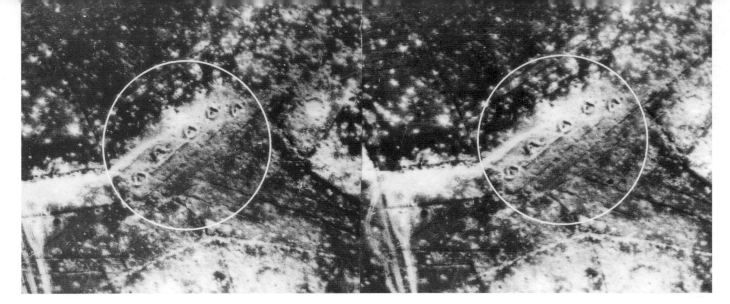

At Cassino, aerial photography backed up what could be seen with considerable ease from ground level. Allied soldiers had a clear view of virtually every move the Germans made, at least in daylight. Movement such as the repositioning of artillery or tanks that would have been easily detected during the day, and consequently result in a hail of fire, was only possible at night. Daylight sorties nevertheless built up a comprehensive film coverage of the contested areas, prints quickly being issued to all interested military units. But there were challenges.

Having camouflaged their strongpoints and heavy weapons so that they were very hard to see from above, the Germans managed to keep much of their firepower from being detected and destroyed by air attack. Although they were repeatedly bombed and strafed, the defenders which included elements of the XIVth Panzer Corps and the 1st Parachute Division, managed not only to hold out but to inflict disproportionately high casualties on the numerically superior international forces opposing them.

THE COURSE OF THE BATTLE

On February 1 a second attempt at a breakout was marginally more successful than the first. A thrust made at the German center carried some Allied troops into the foothills of Cassino before it was beaten back.

With air superiority over the battlefront virtually assured, air and ground commanders alike saw that the sound use of tactical and strategic airpower was the key to breaking the deadlock that developed at Cassino. Destruction of the monastry that dominated the entire battlefield seemed to be a militarily sound move.

Although the Benedictine monastry was strongly believed to be in use by the Germans as

Above: Part of the extensive photo-reconnaissance of German positions—in this case a stereogram—revealed five D-shaped positions for *Nebelwerfer* launchers east of Cassino. Each emplacement housing one of the six-barreled 150mm rocket launchers was about 14ft across.

Right: Typical of the superb clarity obtained by World War II aerial reconnaissance cameras is a general view of Monte Cassino and the Liri Valley taken in March 1944.

a military headquarters, PR coverage had been unable to confirm this without any doubt. The Germans had overseen the packing and removal of all transportable works of art the previous October and tried to persuade the only occupants, the Abbot, five monks and a caretaker staff to leave. They elected to remain.

General Ira Eaker, commanding MAAF and General Jacob Devers, commanding US Sixth Army took the chance to carry out their own air reconnaissance of the monastery and made a low pass at less than 200ft in a Piper Cub. Noticing what he took to be a radio aerial on the monastery roof, Eaker decided that the Germans had indeed had a headquarters inside. This flight was not as risky as it might have seemed, as the Germans generally refrained from shooting at spotter aircraft for fear of subsequent attacks by fighter-bombers. The decision was taken to destroy Monte Cassino to deny its future use by the enemy.

Accordingly on February 15, when the monastery occupants finally chose to leave, 142 heavy and 112 medium bombers dropped 576 tons of high explosive and reduced the historic building to rubble. Artillery fire helped complete the destruction.

On February 16 the 4th Indian Division attacked from the northeast. No impression was made and equal disappointment attended the effort of the 2nd New Zealand Division three

days later. Repercussions as to the merits of bombing Monte Cassino were not slow to emerge; there was much condemnation of the bombing, which seemed at variance with a general Allied policy of avoiding damage to priceless buildings and artifacts in those Italian cities which otherwise harbored tactical targets.

On February 14 the XIVth Panzer Corps had counter-attacked at Anzio and succeeded in pushing the perimeter back about four miles. After a bitter struggle the Germans like the Allies, were forced to dig in and mark time.

Weather then clamped down and for three weeks Cassino was relatively quiet. The Germans had troubles of their own; XIVth Panzer Corps which had defended well against early Allied assaults, now had to marshal its slimmer resources, some of which had been removed to bolster the recent operations that had stopped the Anzio breakout. Allied air operations continued to strike strategic and tactical targets of all kinds and these maintained the slow but sure decimation of the enemy's supplies. It was March 15 before a third ground assault was attempted at Cassino.

The plan was to deploy airpower to literally blast a hole through the German lines. Troops pulled back a thousand yards from Cassino's stone buildings. They waited. Soon the earth in front of them erupted as 275 B-17s and B-24s and some 200 B-25s and B-26s released their loads on the hapless town. It took about three and a half hours to flatten Cassino with 17 different formations of aircraft taking-off from 07.42hrs to 11.30hrs. Including PR and fighter-bomber sorties, MAAF put nearly 1,000 aircraft into the air that day.

At mid-morning, before smoke obscured the target area, PR F-5s made a number of runs over the devastated town. The panoramic post-strike mosiacs they took clearly showed the extent of the damage. The weather forecast was not encouraging and the final photo runs had to be made before overcast also helped hide Cassino from reconnaissance at around midday.

When the dust settled the troops moved cautiously forward—only to be beaten back yet again by intense enemy fire. The Germans had dug themselves in and most of them had been well sheltered from the rain of more than 2,000 demolition bombs. Now they emerged to meet the oncoming Allied tanks with heavy fire. Bulldozers were used to clear the massive heaps of rubble for tanks to move more easily and some ground was taken.

But when heavy rain fell on the night of the 15th, turning the ground into a quagmire and bomb craters into lakes, the advance was obliged to slow down. The weather did not relent and the attack was called off on the 23rd by which time about two-thirds of Cassino was in Allied hands. German troops however, continued to hold the high ground of Monastery Hill, rising 1,700ft above the town.

The Allied high command then unleashed the one instrument of war that the Germans could not stop. Operation "Strangle" set about systematically reducing the flow of supplies to Kesselring's front line positions to a mere trickle. The German commander had 18 divisions at his disposal, half of them facing the most forward Allied positions. These, it was reliably estimated, required a combined total of 4,000 tons of supplies per day. The Germans actually had the capacity to move 80,000 tons every twenty-four hours—if MAAF could reduce that amount significantly, Kesselring would have to give ground.

While the air forces went about "Strangle" from mid-March, attempts were made to get the ground forces moving forward. When the March 15 push came to nothing with the realization that the attacking fronts were too narrow and too easily defended, and the casualty figures out of all proportion to the gains made, Gen Alexander opted for a build up that would be overwhelming under the plan known as Operation "Diadem". He brought up the Eighth Army from the quieter Adriatic area to hold the sector from Cassino across the Liri valley, with the Polish IInd Corps on the right flank and gave Mark Clark's Fifth Army responsibilty for the line from the Liri plain to the coast.

By May 11 Alexander's forces were ready. With fourteen divisions, he was at maximum strength, with the 6th South African Armoured Division in reserve. Even with this weight of men and materiel, which far outweighed anything the Germans could muster in the theater at that time, the initial attack did not go well. The Polish 2nd Corps met stubborn resistance and took many casualties during a week-long assault on Monastry Hill while the advance up the Liri valley gained momentum. The fighting remained bitter but finally the Eighth Army spearheaded the final breakthrough.

Orders were given to withdraw the German Xth Army under von Vietinghoff, a move accepted with great reluctance by the hard-bitten defenders.

As Allied troops slogged up Monastry Hill the Germans still poured fire downward from solid all but impregnable cover, much of it provided by the detonations of Allied bombs, as they gradually abandoned their positions. By the time the first Polish troops set foot on the top of Monastry Hill, the Germans had melted away. It was then May 18.

PERFORMANCE

With the capture of Cassino many lessons were learned in time for similar mistakes not to be repeated in the invasion of Normandy. The early campaign in Italy had taken five months and 105,000 Allied casualties. Among the lessons were that the weather was a factor for which all due allowances had to be made. A source of bitter disappointment to Allied air commanders in Italy, it remained highly unpredictable at best. The elements connived to regularly postpone air operations, reduce the degree of reconnaissance coverage of targets, and generally to result in a lower than planned sortie rate against key targets. On numerous occasions fighters and medium and heavy bombers were adversely affected by poor visibility and solid cloud cover that kept them grounded or disrupted actual tactical operations to the point where to bomb in close proximity to friendly troops was to invite disaster.

Recon sorties over Cassino and the surrounding area had been flown by the aircraft of 90th PRW, the unit composition of which remained little changed for most of 1944. The wing divided its operational flights between target coverage for the 12th and 15th Air Forces and the RAF and, after the Gustav Line was secured, the component squadrons continued to offer outstanding support.

A further air element added to the Allied operational plan at Cassino was the highly successful use of light aircraft such as the Taylorcraft Auster to spot for the guns. Used by

the British Army in an air obervation post role, the pilots of these small, unarmed aircraft passed corrections to gun batteries during bombardments and greatly helped shells to fall where they would be most effective. AOP and its modern equivalent, forward air control, remained an essential element of operations encompassing ground/air co-operation.

The 90th TRW remained in Italy to support 12th and 15th Air Force, its groups being reassigned on October 1. Karl Polifka remained in command and until it returned to the US in April 1945, the wing helped established a photographic library for use in the Mediterranean and European theaters.

Left: German survivors of the battle walk towards Allied positions. Many of the defending troops were surprised at the final order to fall back while they still had ammunition left.

Below: A panorama of Cassino after its capture with the ruins of the town in foreground.

Above Right: A wrecked German 88mm gun and Luftwaffe truck—identified by the prefix letters "WL" on the numberplate—are unheeded by a passing Allied truck and trailer.

Below Right: An Allied convoy passes a shattered Tiger tank on the road to Rome.

OPERATION "OVERLORD"

7 THE D-DAY LANDINGS— JUNE 6, 1944

MISSION AIM

The invasion of Europe, opening of a western front, and liberation of occupied Europe.

BACKGROUND

By 1944 the over-riding situation in every commander's mind was the planned invasion of occupied France. If successful it must surely spell the eventual end of the war. If it failed, that end could be put back by years. Of the many essential facets to be considered, accurate photoreconnaissance would be among the foremost.

A big part of the D-Day build-up was the deception plan. In order to get a toe-hold on the enemy shoreline it was necessary to keep location of the dual landing area a complete secret. It was known through Allied intelligence that the Germans thought the Pas de Calais was the Allies' obvious choice, but the Germans knew too there could be another, anywhere in fact from Cherbourg to the Dutch coast. It suited the Allied planners to let the Germans continue to think the Pas de Calais was a prime area. It therefore became obvious, that any attempt made to favour a specific location would give the game away, so effort against whatever targets that were deemed necessary had to be duplicated along the whole length of Hitler's defensive wall.

German radar sites were just one of the priorities for the combined-ops planners. It would be necessary to blind the Germans in order for the Allied fleet to cross the Channel without detection. These radar sites, similar to the V-1 rocket launch sites that will be referred to in Chapter 10, were small and easily rebuilt or repaired. Therefore, Popular sorties were regularly flown to all known radar installations, just as they were attacked regularly, especially on the run up to D-Day itself. Part of the plan too was to ensure that certain radar sites would be working, those that would need to "see" what the

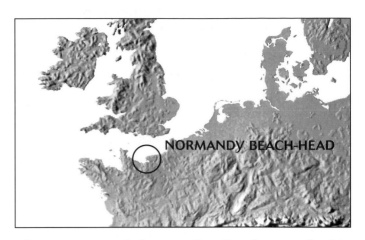

NORMANDY BEACH-HEAD

planners wanted them to "see"—the spoof raids that hopefully would divert German eyes from the invasion area on the Normandy coast. 'Poplars were the code name for a low-level PR sorti, generally using oblique cameras, to bring back photographs of these sites. They would be studied by the PR interpretation people who would determine if they were operational, if they had been attacked, the degree of damage, and how long they might take to become operational once more.

Together with these V-1 and radar tasks, PR aircraft roamed over northern France to check on bridges, roads, railways, and German troop and panzer movements. D-Day planners could never know for certain if their deception plans would work, or if something had leaked out, letting the Germans know that Normandy actually was the invasion point. Therefore one main headache was to guess how quickly the Germans might react to Normandy if they did know, or if they didn't, how quickly could they launch a counter-attack. Once the landings began, it had to be necessary to judge just where any major threat might come from, and along which avenue it might travel. Once established, tactical reconnaissance would be able to pick up troop and panzer movements more easily and be open to attack by either 2nd Tactical Air Force (TAG) fighters and fighterbombers, or medium or heavy bombers from either the RAF or USAAF.

German lines of communications had been a vital target for British and American aircraft since the spring of 1944, disrupting road, rail and river traffic. This had been constant in the weeks leading to the invasion, but one little known operation occurred on May 21 and 22, on which days RAF fighters and fighter-bombers had launched a major effort over France, Belgium and Holland in massed "Rhubarbs" and "Ramrods". It cost the raiders more than 40 fighters but it caused much damage and disruption.

UNITS INVOLVED

The USAAF, too, was heavily involved in this pre-invasion PR including the radar sites. Its three main PR Groups, the 7th, 10th, and 67th each had their tasks. During the pre-invasion period they took oblique photographs of the entire coastal regions from Cherbourg to Holland, assisted by the 25th PR Group (PRG) which operated Mosquito PR XVIs; its CO was Lt-Col Elliott Roosevelt, the second son of the US President.

The 7th Group, 8th Air Force, was commanded by Lt-Col Norris E. Hartwell from May to August 1944, flying the Lockheed F-5 (P-38 Lightning), the distinctive twin-engined, twin-boomed aircraft. The group would receive a Distinguished Unit Citation for its work over the invasion period. The 10th PRG was with the 9th AF, led by Col William B. Reed, with F-6 Mustangs, while the 67th TRG, also with the 9th Air Force, and commanded by Col George W. Peck, also operated with the F-6.

Between May 6 and 20, 1944, the 10th Group was made responsible for vitally important photos of the actual invasion beaches. For these to be of any value for the men who would be streaming ashore on D-Day, they needed to be clear and of good quality, which necessitated low-level sorties. The Americans called these "dicing" missions, as in dicing with death. High- level photographs had indicated beach obstacles but only low-level pictures gave vital clues as to how strong they were and what sort of resistance they would pose to landing-craft and tanks.

Often these low-level sorties would surprise German troops working on these beach defenses, and naturally fearful of being strafed or

Above Right: Low-level oblique photograph of beach obstacles, designed to hinder landing craft at high tide. It was pictures like this that helped persuade planners to land at low tide.

Center Right: Further beach obstacles from low level, this time to seaward. Note shadowy US F-5 Lightning in the foreground. Both these photographs were taken less than three weeks before the invasion on May 19.

Right: More beach obstacles, this time taken by an RAF PR aircraft at low tide. Note the many footprints fom soldiers working on the obstacles.

First Run 0831½ - 0833½.Low water

Line of "Element D" Beach obstacle, calculated Before photography to be 8 feet above Chart Datum. First Run 0832.Low water.

Runnel B beginning to fill up

Bar A dry

bombed, the subsequent photos would show these men running like mad for cover. The pilots not only had to contend with ground fire on these missions, but also sea birds, with which more than one aircraft collided. In the event, the photographs proved so good that even trip-wires attached to mines were detected. Little wonder that the 10th too received a Distinguished Unit Citation for its work at this time. Part of the decision to land at low tide was based on these photos, it being felt better to risk a longer "run up the beach" to losses in troop-laden landing craft hitting these obstacles and booby traps. On D-Day itself the 10th flew 63 missions.

Left: RAF photograph of a French beach taken by a No 140 Squadron aircraft on May 10, 1944, showing obstacles, and high and low sand heights.

Below Left: US photo-interpreters experimented with PR photography of beaches prior to the invasion of Europe so that they would be able to wring every last drop of information from photographs of the D-Day beaches. Here is material taken of Cape Cod, MA, in 1943 identifying features that would be useful on French beaches.

Below: Infra-red and panachromatic photographs of a French port taken by No 140 Squadron RAF on March 23, 1944. The annotation anticipates the depth of water at low tide.

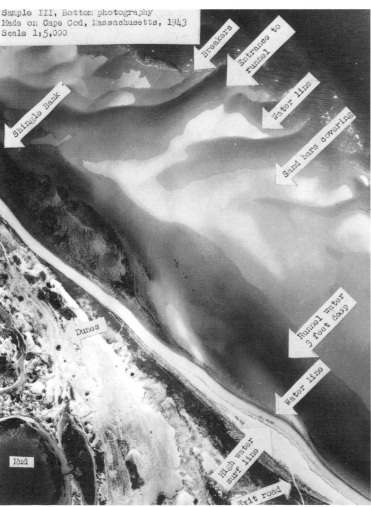

Sample III, Bottom photography Made on Cape Cod, Massachusetts, 1943 Scale 1:5,000

Breakers

Entrance to runnel

Water line

Sand bars covering

Shingle Bank

Dunes

Mud

Runnel water 3 feet deep

Water line

High water surf line

Exit road

4059   KB492.140.23MAR44//RX.H26.38.

INFRA-RED FILM

Very shallow water in the delta, resulting from the flow of the river through the harbor mouth at low tide. Probably not more than 6 inches.

Damp sand left by falling tide shows dark grey.

Panchromatic Fi (same area)

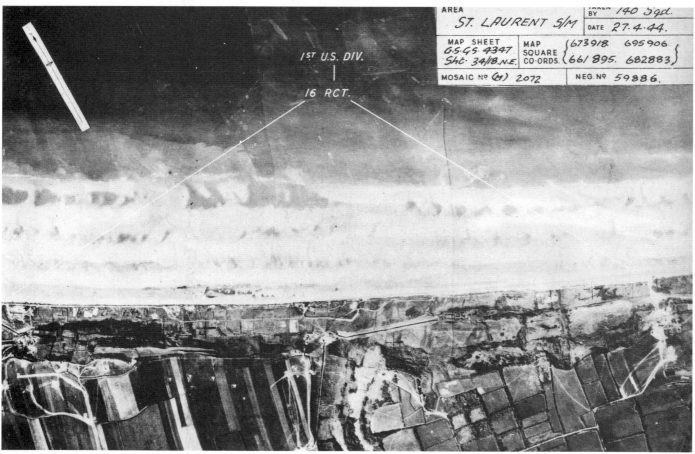

Top: Photograph of St Pierre du Mont taken by the RAF on May 23, 1944, showing the infamous Pointe du Hoc. The landing points for the three companies of Rangers of the 1st US Division are marked. Note the many bomb craters around the area of the supposed heavy gun positions: they had been taken out by the Germans to prevent their destruction by a bombardment. US Rangers discovered them, pointed at "Utah" beach,

ready to fire, in a valley behind Point du Hoc. They were dispatched by Rangers' thermite grenades before they could be used.

Above: A No 140 Squadron photograph of the beaches by St Laurent sur Mer taken on April 27, noted with the landing areas for units of 1st US Division's Rangers.

Above: High level photograph of Vierville sur Mer landing areas for the 1st and 29th US Divisions— "Omaha" Beach.

Right: German engineers run for cover as the low level PR aircraft approaches. Obstacles seen include ramps, stakes and hedge-hogs.

THE COURSE OF THE BATTLE

On D-Day, RAF and USAF aircraft were all affected by the poor weather, not to mention the airfields in waterlogged southern England. The previous day ground crews on RAF and USAAF airfields had been busily painting black and white invasion stripes to wings and fuselages of all aircraft. Luftwaffe reaction could only be guessed at, but at all costs, army and especially navy gunners needed to have instant recognition of friendly and hostile aeroplanes. The black and white stripes became a symbol of the invasion, although for the several allied fighter pilots that were shot down by the navy off the beaches, they must have wondered why they bothered.

The major task for the PR aircraft was to keep the roads to the Normandy coast under keen observation for tanks, armored vehicles and troops. If the Germans did react instantly to the invading forces time would be critical. Fighter-bombers would need to take off and deal with any threat instantly. The problem however, was the weather, but despite this, the pilots were briefed to make every effort to cover all roads leading to the Normandy coast and Caen and to report visually or, whenever possible, photographically any movement they discovered. Success on the beach-head would hinge on swift reactions to any German counter-measure.

Many tasks that were assigned were impossible to carry out due to the low cloud and some rain. Several of the TacR RAF Mustang squadrons were to be used as spotters for the guns of the armada of large warships off the Normandy coast, firing at planned targets or strongpoints that were holding up any advance. Therefore, the TacR element was already reduced.

The first missions were flown by No 69 Squadron RAF with its Wellingtons. Two of these aircraft were out soon after midnight, Flt Sgt P. E. Rushton dropping flares over the road between Rouen and Amiens, while Sqn Ldr K. G. Wakefield dropped flares at Evreux airfield but neither crew saw any activity.

Pre-dawn, Mosquito PR XVIs of No 140 Squadron were out on low-level PR sorties, checking roads etc. in France. Flg Off M. G. Crotty's machine was hit by flak over Amiens, holing its tail, fuel and hydraulic tanks but he got back. Plt Off G. H. Ardley diving to make a low-level run near Amiens lost his cockpit hood as well as meeting light flak. Plt Off J. W. Hall operated between Rouen and Pontoise, and despite intense flak which caused some damage to the machine, brought back valuable photos.

Below: "Omaha" Beach taken at 13.00hrs on D-Day by Maj Smith in an F-5 at 6,000ft. Note the myriad landing craft and vehicles pushing inland on the roads west of Anselles by "Gold" Beach.

84

However, Flg Off F. G. Ruddock and his navigator Flt Sgt H. C. Dent, operating between Mondidier and Cambrai, failed to return.

The landing began at around dawn—06.30 hrs. "Sword," "Juno," and "Gold" were the code names for the British and Canadian landing beaches, east of Bayeux, "Omaha" and "Utah" for the Americans. "Utah" was west of the Carentan inlet, while "Omaha" was to the east, with the Pointe de Hoc overlooking it. Observation from the accompanying ships and from the men on the actual beaches would relay back word of how they were doing, so to directly over-fly the beaches was not wholly required and would be dangerous. PR sorties were generally routed in north or south of them.

The American 7th PRG sent out aircraft at 06.00hrs, flown by Colonel Clarence A. Shoop and Lt-Col Norris Hartwell. Over the Channel they tagged onto a P-38 which they gratefully followed to Normandy. Leaving the Lightning at the coast, they two PR aircraft headed over the beaches under 1,000ft due to low cloud and rain. Completing their task, despite some flak fire, they returned to base at 09.00hrs. Later two operations officers from the 7th, Maj Carl Chapman, and the 8th PRW Lt-Col John Hoover flew a PR mission over the American beaches.

In the afternoon, No 140 Squadron RAF sent an aircraft to photograph the beaches, Sqn Ldr C. D. N. Longley flying over Trouville to St Vaast, meeting light flak at Courseulles but got his pictures. That night Flg Off R. Bastenburg took photos over assigned targets between Lisieux and Pont l'Èveque, then did a visual recce af the roads to St Valery from 200ft. Other Mosquitos went to Nogent-Chartres, Granville-St Lô and Verneuil-Breteuil. These night sorties were flown using GEE but at least one aircraft had its equipment jammed and had to drop its photo-flashes on ETA before taking its low-level photos.

The RAF's No 16 Squadron had the lion's share of PR action on D-Day, beginning with sorties at 07.00hrs but cloud was to be a major problem. PR and TacR became one during the morning as it became necessary to establish troops positions. At 09.05hrs, Wg Cdr C. F. H. Webb, from No 4 Wing HQ, flew a No 16 Squadron Spitfire XI to try and find message strips for the Airborne Division between Quistrehem and Caen, also taking photos of bridges from 1,000ft, but he could find no strips at the expected pin-points. He buzzed the fields in case the soldiers were hiding, but nothing stirred; however he could see that Caen was still in enemy hands. Finally he spotted some "cherry berries" (airborne troops with their maroon berets) in a jeep and dropped a message asking for a location. Collecting the message—written on a map of England—they pointed vaguely south. Webb went south and finally located the strips.

On another No 16 Squadron sortie, Flg Off M. B. Murphy was preparing to photograph Montdidier but spotted a Messerschmitt 109 fighter in his rear-view mirror and climbed into cloud. He then became lost, but photographed activity on a rail line which led him to Amiens.

Another 109 nearly claimed Sqn Ldr E. M. Goodale. It surprised him as he was looking at

Above Left and Above: Allied troops landing on D-Day. Note beachfront houses.

Below: Tank landing craft flying protective balloons off Graye sur Mer ("Gold" Beach) on June 7. Photograph was taken by Lt-Col Norris Hatwell of the 7th US PRG in a Lightning.

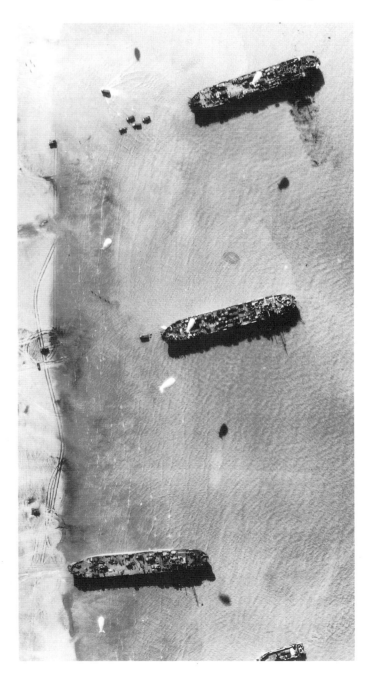

his map, but he evaded it and after ". . . being chased around a bit . . ." was rescued by another Spitfire. Wg Cdr P. Stansfield followed up Webb's strip-finding sortie, found them and made four photo runs from heights of 500ft to 3,000ft.

In the afternoon the No 34 Wing Operations Officer, Flt Lt A. S. Baker, in a No. 16 Squadron Spitfire XI, took obliques of Caen airfield and oblique overlaps of Caen and along the canal, through the glider landing areas. No 4 Squadron had a disappointing day due to the weather. Only Flt Lt D. E. Mobbs in a Spitfire XI made two photo runs over Le Mesnil, west of Amiens during the evening.

The two Canadian squadron too had varied fortune. No 400 Squadron RCAF only managed four Mustang sorties (two pairs) on Popular missions, one pair at 08.35hrs failed due to weather, another pair at 17.55hrs that evening also failed due to weather, although some mosaic pictures were brought back.

However, No 430 Squadron RCAF managed 30 sorties. The first three pairs went out at dawn on purely TacR missions, having lifted off from their rain-soaked airfield while it was still dark. The fourth mission, at 06.00hrs, Flt Lt R. J. H. Taylor and Flg Off R. H. Rohrner covered roads leading to Caen from 6,500ft, taking pictures of motor transport moving towards Caen. The Mustangs carried a camera each, one being a 14in oblique, the other an 8in oblique. Subsequent sorties by No 430 Squadron had the same mix.

Shortly after 07.00hrs, six No. 430 Squadron Mustangs headed out, crossing the French coast at Vierville-sur-Mer, right of "Omaha" Beach, then swept round to the east to cover roads from Bayeux to Caen, but saw nothing at first. Then they photographed some Major Vehicle Traffic

Left: A high altitude oblique photograph from the French coast off "Gold" Beach on D-Day, taken by Capt Cassady from 2,000ft.

(MT) and possibly two tanks south-west of Bayeux. At 08.45hrs two pairs crossed in at Port en Bessin, to the left of "Omaha," checking along the road from the Port to Bayeux from 2,000ft. They met flak and saw some tanks and AFVs which their cameras picked up.

Another pair of Canadians went out at 11.00hrs along the roads north of Caen to Falaise, Agentan, Mortagne, Alençon, and Domfort. Two more pairs followed shortly afterwards via Port Bessin, spotted some MT and were fired at by flak gunners on Caen airfield.

At 15.00hrs Flg Offs W. P. Golden and T. H. Lambros checked the roads from Le Mans-Alençon-Domfort and Vieville. They saw six Ju88 bombers near the coast but they had more serious work to do. They photographed the bombed bridge at Villiers. At 16.35hrs, Wg Cdr J. M. Godfrey (from No 126 Airfield) with Flg Off J. S. Cox, flew as cover escort to three PR Mustangs covering the roads from Montfort to Evreux. Movement seen almost at once but they were immediately intercepted by six FW190 fighters, and Cox was shot down. (He was possibly the sole P-51 claimed by JG26 this day.) Godfrey, Sqn Ldr F. H. Chesters, No 430's CO, and the others were chased back to the coast. No 430's last sorties of D-Day were TacR sorties.

No 34 PR Wing, whose HQ was at Northolt, flew 28 sorties on D-Day, including the five night sorties. D-Day proved a magnet for several senior air force officers in various commands, and not least PR. Among those who flew on D-Day were Grp Capt P. B. B. Oglivie DSO, DFC, (famed earlier for taking the first recce photos of Berlin) a successful sortie in a Spitfire PR XI, and Air Cdre A. J. W. Geddes DSO, the DSASO of 2nd TAF who made another successful recce in a Mustang. He had his own highly polished P-51 fitted with 8in cameras. He flew over the British and Canadian beaches at 800-1,000ft, providing the first pictures of the landings.

However, as Geddes approached the Cherbourg peninsula he could not see any penetration of troops beyond the beach. This proved to be "Omaha" Beach on which the 116th US Infantry was desperately trying to hang on to their toe-hold. His report was of much value. The other beach landings were slowly pushing inland, but "Omaha" was causing problems and being near the centre, it was vital it did not fail. The PR aircraft kept a close watch on the area inland but luckily the Americans finally broke out, fortunate that no strong counter move by the Germans was made. Had it been, the PR boys would have picked it up, heralding air attacks by Typhoons.

PERFORMANCE

There was also a victory for the recce pilots. Lt Joe Conklin of the 15th TacR Squadron, soon to be part of the 10th PRG shot down a FW190 near Dreux, west of Paris, the first kill of D-Day. But it was not all one-sided. The Americans lost two Mustangs from the 67th TacR Group, while the 7th PRG lost one F-5.

Despite the weather, the day proved of worth and value to the PR pilots. They had, in the main, carried out their vital role behind the beaches, and would continue to do so for the next several days, for at any time the Germans might push up their Panzers. As the invasion forces headed inland, equally vital sorties lay in store for the cameras of the low-level Mustangs, Spitfires, F-5s, and F-6s.

Below: Mulberry Harbour, June 22, 1944. Note the mass of landing craft and stores on the shoreline and trucks heading inland on the roads.

Bottom: Mulberry Harbour, June 17, 1944, taken by Flg Off Reeves in a Spitfire from 30,000ft. The "breakwater" consists of merchantmen and old warships anchored, while special pontoons make up piers and jetties.

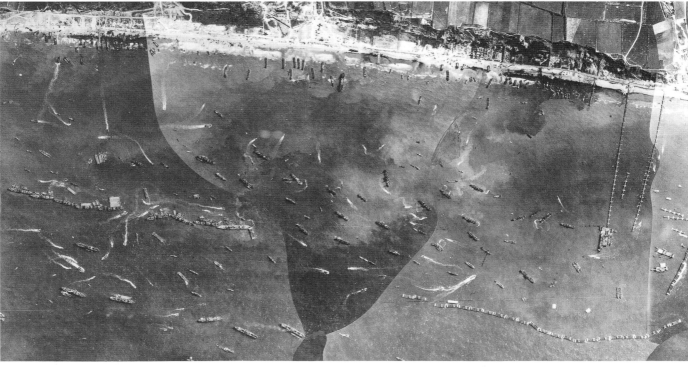

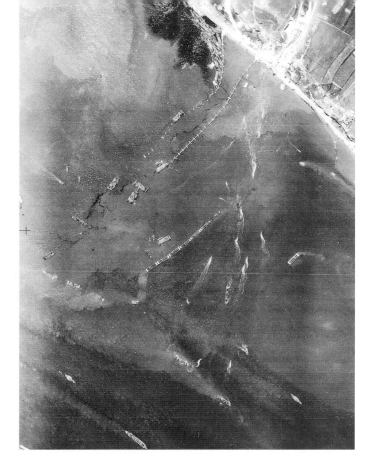

Above and Above Left: Sections of Mulberry taken on June 24.

Left: An oblique view of Mulberry looking to the southwest.

Below Left: A map of the staging areas for Mulberry prior to D-Day. From these ports the mighty artificial harbor would be taken across to the Normandy coast for assembly.

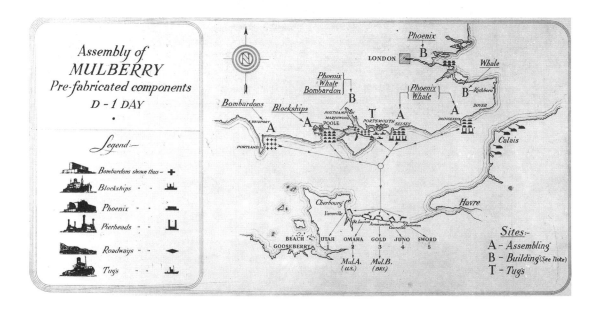

"GOODWOOD" & "COBRA"

8 THE NORMANDY BREAKOUT, JULY 18—AUGUST 26, 1944

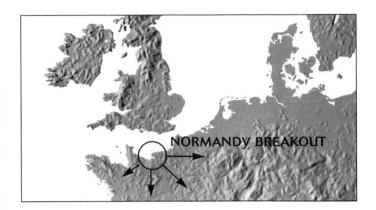

NORMANDY BREAKOUT

MISSION AIM

The breakout from the D-Day bridgehead and the *bocage* country.

BACKGROUND

Following the successful establishment of a bridgehead ashore, the allied plan of campaign involved a British advance on Caen (Operation "Goodwood"), which would draw in most of the German panzer forces enabling the Americans on the allied right to envelop the enemy in a wheeling movement south and east (Operation "Cobra"). However, ever since D-Day the Allied armies had been restricted to an attritional infantry slogging match in Normandy's *bocage* countryside, a hedgerow-by-hedgerow, field-by-field, building-by-building rooting out of a well-entrenched enemy. Pushing inland from the beaches was almost entirely infantry work. Although faced with a disturbing dilemma—that the Normandy stalemate was eating into Allied infantry reserves and it was infantry that would be required to break

the deadlock—the overall commander on the ground, General Montgomery, adopted an aggressive strategy. The base of the Cotentin peninsula was cut on June 17 and Cherbourg fell by June 27. In Operation "Epsom" the British advanced to the Odon river and by July 9 in Operation "Charnwood" British and Canadian infantry had secured Caen's suburbs. However, in order to successfully pivot the Americans and sweep east Montgomery would have to hold the Caen-Falaise plain. He had no option but to launch another assault on Caen and "hoped that 'Goodwood' would be the last big Anglo-Canadian effort in Normandy before the break-out, and that it should be a battle of material rather than men."

Below: Spitfire XIs preparing to sortie over the Channel to France.

UNITS INVOLVED

Above: British armor advances in the build-up to "Goodwood." Fighting in the *bocage* country of Normandy was demanding on tanks and tank crews and made for slow progress.

Photographic and tactical reconnaissance missions for the Allied armies were provided by the Allied Expeditionary Air Force (AEAF) which consisted of Maj-Gen Quesada's 9th US TAF and AVM Broadhurst's 2nd British TAF. The latter consisted of a Headquarters Section as well as two groups; No 83 Group which supported British Second Army, and No 84 Group which supported Canadian First Army. Each of the these had a PR wing attached. The HQ Section had No 34 Wing which comprised No 16 Squadron RAF (Spitfire IXs and XIs), No 69 Squadron RAF (Wellington XIIIs), and No 140 Squadron RAF (Mosquito IXs and XVIs). No 35 Wing RAF formed part of No 84 Group and comprised No 2 Squadron RAF (Mustangs), No 4 Squadron RAF (Spitfire XIs) and No 268 Squadron RAF (Mustangs). No 39 Wing RAF came under No 83 Group and was formed of No 168 Squadron RAF (Mustangs), No 400 Squadron RCAF (Spitfires, Mosquitos), No 414 Squadron RAF (Mustangs) and No 430 Squadron RCAF (Mustangs).

The real mainstays of the British PR effort throughout the campaign were the Spitfire and the Mosquito. It was fortunate for the Allies that they were vastly superior to anything the Germans had, because the photo-intelligence that they provided was one of the keys to success not just in this particular campaign, but throughout the war. Nos 35 and 39 PR Wings supplied close tactical support to the armies while they were still caged in their Normandy bridgeheads. The armies were greatly relieved to have almost immediate photographic evidence of enemy troops and positions supplied by the

RAF. In *Eyes of the RAF* Roy Conyers Nesbit says, "sorties were usually of short duration and the pilots gave R/T reports while in the air, followed by immediate interrogation on landing. Their photographs were rapidly printed by an MFPS [Mobile Field Photographic Sections] and photocopies were circulated to the troops, even down to platoon level." The American element consisted of one Tactical Reconnaissance Group (TRG) and one Photographic Reconnaissance Group (PRG). One was assigned to each of the two Tactical Air Commands (TAC) that comprised Quesada's 9th US Air Force. Col George W. Peck commanded the 67th TRG flying North American F-6s (P-51D Mustangs) under IXth TAC, and Col William B. Reed commanded 10th PRG which flew Lockheed F-5s (P-38G and H Lightnings) under XIXth TAC. The 67th TRG had a strength of four squadrons, the 12th, 15th, 107th, and 109th Tactical Reconnaissnce Squadrons. The 10th PRG comprised three Photographic Reconnaissance Squadrons, the 30th, 33rd, and 34th.

The distinction between Tactical Reconnaissance Squadrons and Photographic Reconnaissance Squadrons requires some amplification, as each fulfilled marginally differing roles. In *World War Two Photo Intelligence* Col R. M. Stanley states that the PR squadrons were "pure" aerial photographers flying unarmed F-5s. TRS aircraft, usually F-6s, kept their guns and were used for photo or visual recon. Some of the TacR pilots shot down enemy aircraft, and they often flew "armed reconnaissance" missions in flights of

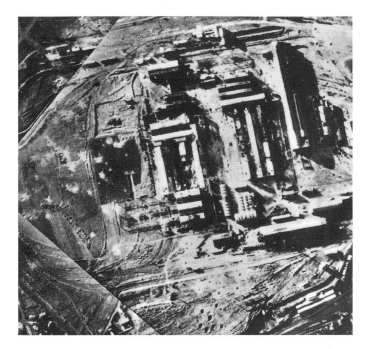
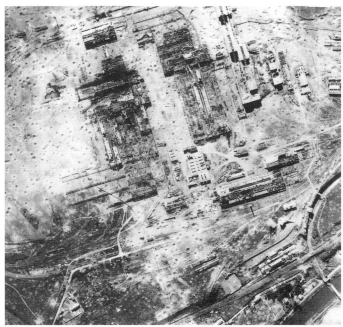

Above Left and Above: Collombelles steel factory before and after the morning raid on July 18, 1944, the day "Goodwood" started.

twos or fours during which they shot up anything they saw worth attacking and then reported it later. Photographic sorties accounted for roughly 10 percent of the combat flights by 9th Air Force TRSs.

In accordance with the "Transportation Plan" aimed at destroying German communications, the PR units played a crucial role, tactically and strategically, in denying the enemy the ability to move forces speedily into Normandy. By the time of the D-Day landings, all the bridges over the River Seine below Paris had been destroyed as a part of this strategy. Nesbit says,

"Throughout the battle for France enormous efforts were made by the Germans to repair or replace the bridges, and air reconnaissance missions, photographic and tactical, became an important factor in the battle to keep the bridges closed." For example, on July 18, the day "Goodwood" went in, Flg Off E. J. Geddes of No 430 Squadron RCAF flew a PR mission between 18.20hrs and 18.50hrs over the bridges between Thury Harcourt and Caen in Mustang AP178J, reporting, "Bridge at U.2167 completely destroyed, three more out, one repaired, two intact with approaches damaged. Slight inaccurate flak from Thury Harcourt area."

Towards the end of the battle, when the breakout had become a race to reach the Seine, the continued destruction of the bridges and the engineer units undertaking repair work greatly impaired the German retreat. Sqn Ldr Ellis of No 400 Squadron RCAF flew a PR mission the length of the Seine bridges on August 19 and his

report attests to the traffic congestion facing the fleeing German Army caused by the "bridges" policy–"Motorized Enemy Transport bumper to bumper for two miles." The Allied TAFs won the war of the bridges only by maintaining daily reconnaissance missions along the length of the rivers in northern France.

"Following the Normandy breakout, ground units virtually outran their tactical photo intelligence capabilities. Territory was being taken so fast that film processing and readout were frequently too slow." This directly led to the preponderence of combined visual and armed reconnaissance missions in the campaign as the 2nd and 9th Tactical Air Force reconnaissance units leapfrogged their way across France and up into the Low Countries in the wake of 12th American and 21st British Army Groups.

"GOODWOOD"

"Goodwood," like its predecessor. would open with a massive aerial bombardment; 1,900 bombers dropping 6,858 tons of bombs. The use of "aerial artillery" was taken to extremes in the Normandy campaign. The softening up of ground objectives by "carpet bombing" before an attack was launched involved bombers flying

in a close box formation and pulverizing the target with a massive concentration of bombs.

Operation "Goodwood" was an armored thrust towards the heart of Normandy launched on July 18 from the bridgehead east of Ranville. The VIIIth Corps was to spearhead the attack with three armored divisions. To start the attack three double Bailey bridges over the Orne and the Caen canal had to be crossed, in full view of the Germans perched on the tall chimneys of the Colombelles steel factory at Caen. Five miles south of Caen rose the high ground of Bourguebus, which gave the Germans perfect observation of the British advance, and excellent fields of fire for their artillery. A further handicap was that the British artillery would remain west of the River Orne until all the armor had crossed the three bridges, and even then moving the guns forward would produce a nightmare

Top: Typical post-D-Day aerial operations involved the supression of all German reinforcements, who had a torrid time reaching the coastal areas. Allied air supremacy over the battlefield would be a telling factor in the subsequent operations.

Above: Caen received a terrible hammering: this is all that is left of the market square on July 7.

traffic problem. Montgomery was counting on his overwhelming air support to redress the odds which were against him. The initial effect of the bombing had been stunning. However, not all the defenses were engulfed for two Mustangs of No 268 Squadron RAF noted that the returning bombers were "being subjected to intense flak." In the wake of the explosive carpet, tanks were turned upside down and infantry positions just disappeared in the blast with no traces of their occupants remaining, but the Germans fought on, demonstrating once again the strength of their fighting spirit. Unfortunately, though, the German artillery positions were omitted from the Allied bombing program, so that the hapless armored infantry of 11th Armored Division got bogged down as soon as they encountered enemy infantry blocking positions out of range of friendly guns but ably supported by their own artillery. Additionally, because of the traffic queues, the armored infantry could not keep up with the tanks and were soon left far behind in mopping up operations.

In the event, "Goodwood" was not the decisive battle that was hoped for, being heavily defeated by a force of well deployed tanks and anti-tank guns sited on the Bourguebus ridge. Largely denied infantry support, the tanks had to advance on a one-squadron front—the motorized infantry went forward in lorries which offered no protection to their passengers whatsoever. The nature of the terrain would have resulted in a series of bloody massacres for the infantry battalions had they been employed large scale. Under devastating tank and anti-tank fire, the advance came to a halt. By mid-morning the Panther battalion of the 1st SS Panzer Regiment launched a counter-attack which destroyed the British armor wholesale.

Below: Advanced British infantry elements enter Caen prior to "Goodwood."

From 11.00hrs onwards a tank battle raged-which defied description. At times the Panzers were only kept at bay by rocket-firing Typhoons although there was a general lack of tactical air support.

Matters were not helped by the fact that the tank carrying the 11th Division's RAF Forward Air Controller was taken out within two hours. By the end of the day the 11th Armoured Division, which spearheaded the operation, was reduced to less than 50 percent of its tank establishment. Although it achieved one of its primary aims (drawing the bulk of the German armor onto the Caen "hinge," enabling the US First Army to break out of the bridgehead in the west), a very heavy price was paid in tanks.

However, the Germans had been stretched to breaking point by "Goodwood." Their right flank was now very vulnerable, and to strengthen it the Germans had to commit the very panzer divisions they were soon to need 35 miles to the west to stop Bradley's breakout attempt.

COBRA AND THE BREAKOUT

Having finally captured St Lô by July 19—with 11,000 casualties—Bradley next put into operation the long awaited breakout, "Cobra." The US First Army would advance to Avranches and open the door to Brittany; then Patton's newly constituted Third Army would pass through the gap and race for the vital Breton ports. Even Montgomery was optimistic; Ultra signals showed the Germans in the US sector to be in poor shape, and confirmed that "Goodwood" had drawn almost all the German armor onto the British front, so that American prospects for "Cobra" were excellent.

Bradley opted for "Cobra" to be spearheaded by three infantry divisions, holding his armor in reserve. It was to begin on July 24 being preceeded by an aerial bombardment of 1,887 bombers and 529 fighters, but bad weather forced a one-day postponement. Unfortunately, 350 bombers did not receive this order and proceeded, mistakenly, to drop some of their ordnance on US 30th Infantry Division killing 25 and wounding 131. Next day some of the bombers repeated their mistake and 111 soldiers were killed, including Lt-Gen Lesley McNair, the highest ranking Allied officer to be killed in northwest Europe. The commander of the hap-

Above: US M4 Mediums—Shermans—move south towards Avranches on July 29.

Left: Elements of US 6th Armored Division pass a soldier of 30 Commando on July 28.

Below Left: US troops escort German prisoners in Brehal, July 30.

Bottom Left: French civilians flock to greet their liberators at Granville, at the bottom of the Cotentin Peninsula, July 31.

less 30th Division, which was hit for the second day running, described it as, "horrible. The ground belched, shook and spewed dirt to the sky. Scores of our troops were hit, their bodies flung from the slit trenches. Dazed and frightened doughboys were quivering in their holes."

US VIIth Corps made little progress, the infantry were demoralized after two days of "blue-on-blue" engagements, and the German artillery that the bombers were supposed to have suppressed opened fire laying down a devastating barrage in the path of the advancing Americans. This was indeed unfortunate for the Americans as Fritz Bayerlein's Panzer Lehr Division was the principal armored formation facing Bradley and it only had 15 tanks left in reserve!

However, by July 27 General Collins (VIIth Corps) realized that he was facing a shattered enemy, not the layered defenses that Rommel had deployed to blunt "Goodwood." He took a gamble that paid off and committed two of his armored formations to battle early. Additionally, with VIIIth Corps joining the battle on VIIth Corps' right flank, sufficient pressure was applied to the brittle enemy line that it soon became simply a matter of time before "American armor began to outflank the defensive positions and seize crossroads in their rear to prevent the Germans from escaping with their materiel." The vital crossroads town of

Coutances fell into American hands on July 28. The situation was perfect for exploitation.

Bradley decided to unleash Patton. The Germans could not put in an armored counter-attack to prevent disaster here because six of their Panzer divisions were still facing the British. "The American generals in the field were sincere in their gratitude to Montgomery for diverting so much German armor to the east. His plan to hold the enemy in the British sector now paid huge dividends. As the key road junction at Avranches fell on August 1, Patton's Third Army HQ came into operation and his divisions, freed of the risk of heavy German counter-attacks, streamed into Brittany."

THE FALAISE "GAP"

On August 6, Monty, with Bradley in total agreement, ordered Patton to "pivot on our left and swing hard with our right along the southern flank and in towards Paris to drive the enemy up against the River Seine." By August 8 Le Mans fell; by the 13th, Alençon. Patton's troops now formed a huge bulge east of Brittany, which at its northern edge represented the bottom half of a huge pincer. Dempsey's British forces, slowly advancing south of Caen, formed the top half. On July 30 Dempsey ordered VIIIth and XXXth Corps to attack south from

Caumont in Operation "Bluecoat," and they successfully drove a deep wedge between German Seventh and Fifth Armies, having been instructed by Montgomery that "all caution [is] to be thrown overboard, every risk [is] to be taken, and all troops [are] to be told to put everything into it." With Patton's armor pouring into France, the Germans launched a counter-stroke at Mortain on August 6 in an attempt to sever the Cotentin peninsula.

Monty "put the whole of 2nd Tactical Air Force on to deal with the attacks," and by August 8 it was halted. By the time the Canadians reached Falaise on August 17, Patton's XVth Corps had been at Argentan the best part of five days. Bradley ordered Patton to halt, writing in his memoirs that he preferred "a solid shoulder at Argentan to a broken neck at Falaise."

"In the haze, the smoke and the dust of this violent, closely engaged battle, a collision between ground forces would indeed have become a menacing reality with each step that they took towards each other." To have driven into the British advance could have produced disastrous errors of recognition. Montgomery had prohibited bombing in the area because of the heavy casualties suffered by 21st Army Group from Allied bombers. 51st Highland Division complained of 40 incidents of blue-on-blue on August 18, with 25 vehicle casualties

Right: Map showing Allied ground forces involved in the Falaise Gap battles. The German Army was thoroughly defeated as a conclusion to the Normandy invasion. As their forces streamed back through northern France and the Low Countries, much the way they had entered some four years earlier, the Gestapo was rounding up the generals implicated in the July 20 bomb plot. The end of the war beckoned.

and 51 personnel. The division's report stated: "Continual bombing by our own forces. Half the petrol being sent to 2nd Armoured destroyed. During a three-day period 72 Polish soldiers were killed and 191 wounded: the Canadians lost 77 killed and 209 wounded from own bombing." The nearness of the two armies would have made tactical bombing impractical, but there were plenty of targets for the air forces to the east and west of the bottleneck.

Flt Lt Richard Rohmer, a Canadian pilot, flew a reconnaissance mission over the "Gap" on August 19. Crossing the main road to Falaise three miles north of Argentan, he noted, "There was before me in a long double line stretching westward the largest, most valuable 'target of opportunity' I had or ever would see . . . The order prohibiting air attacks in the Falaise Gap was in force . . . two days later in a jeep I went down the four miles of road . . . there was not a single destroyed or damaged vehicle.

On August 20 the Poles finally sealed the "Gap" and their artillery wrought havoc on the dense slow moving columns of retreating Germans. A counter-attack briefly re-opened the "Gap" but by August 22 it was finally sealed. 10,000 Germans are known to have died in that barrage, and a further 50,000 became prisoner of war in the "Gap."

PERFORMANCE

The battle did go broadly according to plan. Bradley, like Montgomery, saw "Goodwood" as a preliminary to "Cobra," and considered the two operations should be judged together. Bradley's 12th Army Group spearheaded by Patton broke through the Avranches gap and penetrated deep into Brittany. By mid-August, British, Canadian, and US forces in the north and Patton's forces sweeping round to the south had encircled the German forces between Falaise and Argentan, creating the "Falaise Gap."

Allied PR units played a significant role aiding the armies throughout the entire campaign, especially so in keeping the bridges down. Despite the destruction of the bridges, the Germans were able to activate ferries so that by August 19 when the Allies had reached the west bank the bulk had been ferried across and raced out of France to the more easily defensible Low Countries and Alsace-Lorraine.

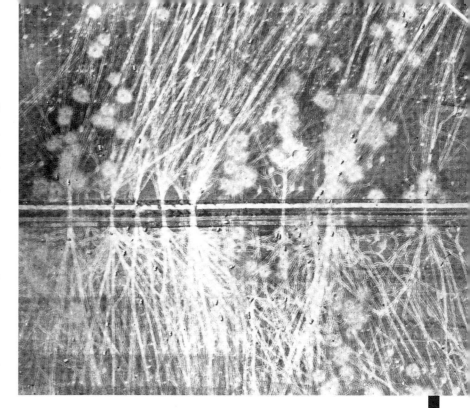

Above: Allied units cross a main road following in the tracks of the fleeing Germans. The proximity of the two armies led to numerous blue-on-blue engagements.

Below: Allied PR on the bridges ensured they were bombed as soon as they were rebuilt. This is at Port du Gravière between Rouen and Paris.

Nevertheless, in strategic terms, a decisive victory had been won as great as any the Russians had achieved in the east. German losses in Normandy totalled 450,000 men including 210,000 prisoners, compared to Allied losses of 209,672, of which 36,976 were killed

"BODYLINE" & "CROSSBOW"

9 FINDING AND DESTROYING THE V-WEAPONS

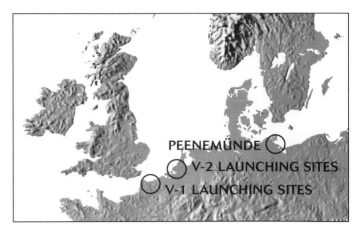

MISSION AIM

To locate with the aid of PR the development installations and launch sites for Hitler's V-weapons program in Germany and France. Then to destroy through bombing the German V-weapons program, thereby saving London and other English cities from destruction, and preventing disruption to the build-up of men and materiel in southern England prior to the Allied invasion of Normandy in June 1944.

BACKGROUND

In the week following the Allied landings on the northern coast of France in June 1944, the Nazis finally unleashed the first of their *Vergeltung* or vengeance weapons against England in retaliation for the massive damage being caused to Germany by the Allied Combined Bomber Offensive. A series of delays had prevented them from bringing the V-1 flying bomb into use the previous autumn, their intention being to bombard London from dozens of launch sites along the northern coast of France with 3,000 missiles a day until the complete devastation of the British capital was assured.

The V-1 was a small unmanned aircraft that carried a 1,800lb high explosive warhead and was powered by a single pulse jet engine that propelled it at speeds of up to 500mph, faster than any fighter aircraft possessed by the Allies. Although the plans to use the V-1 were delayed thanks to the combined efforts of the RAF's PR pilots, the CIU staff at RAF Medmenham, and the bomber pilots of the RAF and USAAF, the bombardment of southern England by flying bombs eventually went ahead.

Far more sinister and potentially deadlier than the subsonic V-1, the second of Hitler's vengeance weapons was the V-2 rocket. Powered by a liquid-fueled rocket motor, it was packed with high explosive and flew to its target at more than five times the speed of sound. The first sign of its arrival from out of the stratosphere was the explosion when it hit the ground and its warhead detonated, followed moments later by the roar of its arrival. Only now is it becoming clear that a special version of the V-2 was intended to carry a far more lethal payload than simply high explosive. New evidence points to plans for a

Right: Flying bombs wreak havoc on London's docklands. Without the delays caused to the German V-weapons program by Allied bombing, this romanticized artist's impression of a V-1 salvo over the British capital could have become a reality. (From a Dutch edition of the German Army Propaganda magazine *Signal.*)

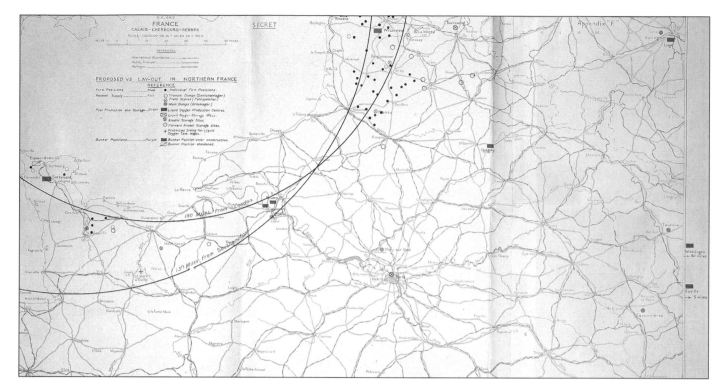

Above: Intensive photo-reconnaissance of the coast of northern France and its hinterland enabled British intelligence to build a picture of proposed V-2 rocket sites, their storage, and supply infrastructure.

irradiated dust to be carried in the payload bay of the rocket, which would be detonated in the skies above urban areas like London and Bristol, and as far away as the eastern seaboard of the US, spreading clouds of radioactive contamination in the air to kill thousands of people. That the Germans did not use this terrifying radioactive alternative to high explosive is more down to chance than due to any intervention on the part of the Allies.

Ranged against this formidable arsenal of terror weapons, the RAF could field five photo-reconnaissance squadrons equipped mainly with PR Spitfires and Mosquitoes, with one squadron based at Leuchars in Scotland, and the remainder at Benson in Oxfordshire. One PR Mosquito squadron based at San Severo in Italy was also utilised for long-range PR sorties over Poland. The USAAF had four PR squadrons based at Mount Farm, close to Benson, equipped with the P-38, F-4, and F-5, and a handful of PR Spitfires.

The offensive element of the Allied air forces comprised the whole combined might of RAF Bomber Command using the Lancaster, Halifax, Stirling, Mosquito, and Wellington, and the US 8th Air Force's VIIIth Bomber Command with the B-17 and B-24, which were made available to bomb V-weapon targets. From May 1943, the fighter-bomber and medium bombers of the RAF's 2nd Tactical Air Force and the US 9th Air Force were also active, using the A-20 Boston, B-25 Mitchell, B-26 Marauder, Typhoon, and Tempest.

THE COURSE OF THE BATTLE

Reports of secret weapon trials on the north German coast at a place called Peenemünde were known to British Intelligence as early as the autumn of 1939, but the so-called "Oslo Report" that gave details of long range weapons, including rockets, was filed away for future reference.

It was not until a routine sortie over northern Germany on May 15, 1942 by a lone Spitfire of No 1 PRU flown by Flt Lt D. W. Steventon brought back photographs of Peenemünde airfield on the Baltic coast, that Intelligence began to sit up and take notice. The photographs revealed feverish construction activity that included three strange-looking circular emplacements on the ground, but nothing that struck Medmenham's photographic interpreters as out of the ordinary. Later that year intelligence reports received from Allied agents indicated that the Germans had recently test-fired rockets at Peenemünde, but further reconnaissance sorties on January 19 and March 1 could reveal nothing to link the building activity with long-range rockets.

In March 1943, secretly taped conversations between two captured German generals confirmed British suspicions that the Germans were

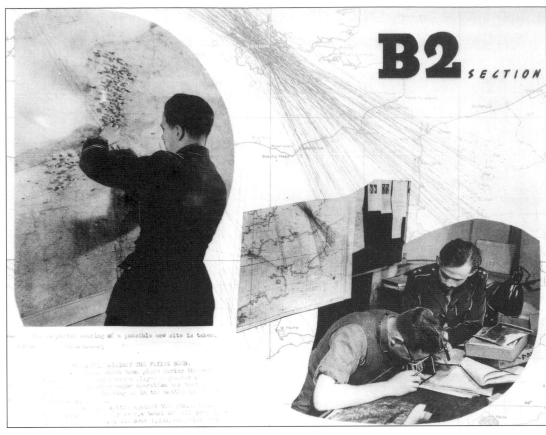

B2 SECTION

Left: Photographic interpreters worked round the clock at the Central Interpretation Unit (CIU) at Medmenham, in the Thames valley, to unravel the secrets of the German V-weapons program before it was too late.

Below: An example of the detailed target map provided to Bomber Command's aircrews for their precision night attack on the German research establishment at Peenemünde on the Baltic, August 17/18, 1943.

involved in a rocket building program, and more PR was ordered for Peenemünde. At the same time a special flying program was instituted to cover every square mile of the French coast from Cherbourg to the Belgian border to look out for potential launch sites. It was shared between the RAF's PR squadrons at Leuchars (No 540 Squadron), at Benson (Nos 541, 542, 543, and 544 Squadrons), and the US 8th Air Force at nearby Mount Farm (13th, 14th, and 22nd PR Squadrons. A fourth squadron, No 27 PR, became operational in November).

The first confirmation of rocket building at Peenemünde came in a can of film shot on May 14 by a PR Mosquito of No. 540 Squadron flown by Sqn Ldr Gordon Hughes from Leuchars which, under close scrutiny, revealed vehicles carrying unidentifiable long cylindrical objects. Further sorties added more detail until; on June 12, the first definite sighting of a rocket was made, lying on a trailer near to a building and close by one of the circular emplacements. An unidentifiable thick vertical column reckoned to be about 40ft high was also observed, but for the time being these objects were not recognised as rockets.

Meanwhile, PR coverage of the French coast by Spitfires of No. 542 Squadron was bearing fruit. Interpreters discovered that work was proceeding on a huge concrete structure at Watten

near Calais, as well as at two other locations nearby, and all served by railway lines. Duncan Sandys, then Joint Parliamentary Secretary to the Ministry of Supply, was given the important task of co-ordinating the investigation into the secret weapon threat codenamed "Bodyline" and, acting on his conclusion that the situation was becoming so serious, the Chiefs of Staff ordered Peenemünde to be bombed.

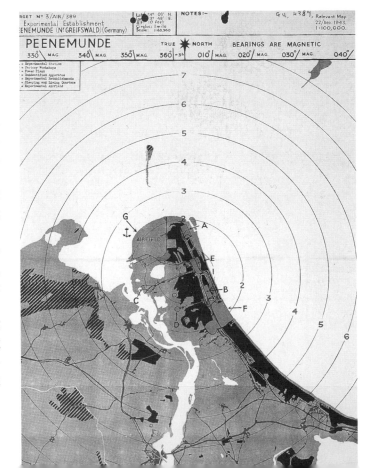

In bright moonlight on the night of August 17, Bomber Command launched a maximum effort raid by 560 heavy bombers on the German research establishment, causing severe damage and setting back the V-2 experimental programme by at least two months. Forty bombers were lost. Post-raid reconnaissance confirmed that substantial damage had been caused to the Peenemünde site. The raid was also important to the RAF because it was the only occasion during the second half of the war on which a maximum effort was launched at night by Bomber Command against a small precision target. It was also the first time that the Pathfinder Force used the Master Bomber technique where one aircraft controlled the progress of the whole raid while orbiting above the target area.

Ten days later, on August 27, 224 B-17 Fortress aircraft of the US 8th Air Force's 1st and 4th Bomb Wings bombed Watten. The Germans had just laid tons of concrete at the V-2 launching site, which was still wet when the bombs came raining down. Within a few days the concrete had hardened, setting in a rigid mass the chaos and destruction caused by the bombing. Damage assessment photographs later showed it would have been quicker for the Germans to start all over again than attempt to effect repairs.

Sinister new building activity continued to be observed by PR sorties over the Pas de Calais and in the vicinity of Cherbourg. On October 21, Duncan Sandys ordered that a comprehensive flying program involving a hundred or more sorties should be flown without delay to re-photograph the whole area under suspicion. The interpreters at Medmenham were kept very busy during the first week in November searching for rail-served rocket launching sites on the thousands of prints. So far, they believed they were only looking for one secret weapon, a rocket.

A new discovery was made on November 3 when eight sites in the Pas de Calais area were photographed after intelligence received from an agent in France described the construction of sites suspected to be for secret weapons. Analysis of the prints revealed no railways nearby or evidence of any new rail spurs leading to the sites, but the buildings bore a striking resemblance to giant skis laid down on their sides and were obviously intended for launching something, but probably not rockets. As November wore on, more of these so-called "ski sites" sites were being identified by PR pilots of No 541

Portion Enlarged.

Left: Before and after the attack by 560 RAF heavy bombers: the main manufacturing and experimental section at Peenemünde.

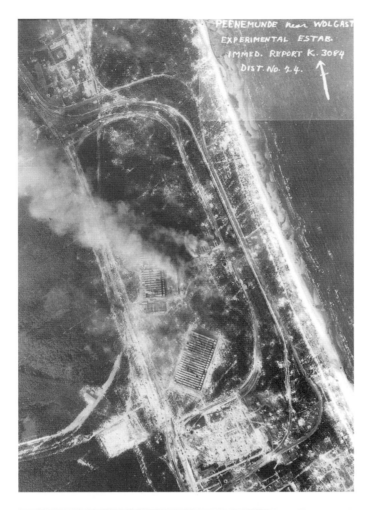

PEENEMÜNDE near WOLGAST
EXPERIMENTAL ESTAB.
IMMED. REPORT K. 3084
DIST. No. 24.

Left: B-17 Flying Fortress aircraft of the US 8th Air Force's 1st Bombardment Division attacked Peenemünde by day on August 4, and again on the 25th. PR sorties for damage assessment were flown from Mount Farm, Oxfordshire, by F-5s of No 27 (PR) Squadron.

Squadron on almost a daily basis. By the end of the month no fewer than 95 had been discovered, mainly in the Pas de Calais and aimed at London, but there were also clusters further west near Cherbourg, pointing towards Bristol and Plymouth.

At this stage in the investigation there were two schools of thought about the German secret weapons program in British Intelligence circles: one led by Duncan Sandys favored long-range rockets, while the other, which included among its supporters the Prime Minister's scientific adviser Lord Cherwell, favored pilotless aircraft. Matters had reached such an impasse that Winston Churchill was forced to appoint Sir Stafford Cripps to examine all the available evidence and decide whether the German secret weapons really existed, and if so what they were and the level of threat they posed. In his report submitted to the War Cabinet in mid-November, Sir Stafford Cripps advised that pilotless aircraft were likely to pose a more immediate threat than long-range rockets, but that PR of Peenemünde and the French coast should be maintained.

On November 28, 1943, returning from an abortive photo-recce sortie to Berlin in a Mosquito PR IX of No 540 Squadron, Sqn Ldr John Merifield overflew the airfield at Peenemünde and a radar installation close by at Zinnowitz on the island of Usedom, and switched on his cameras. The pictures he brought home were to provide the crucial link between the ski sites in France and the existence of a second secret weapon in the form of a pilotless aircraft, the V-1 flying bomb. Flt Off Constance Babington Smith and Wg Cdr Douglas Kendall, both of whom were expert photo-interpreters at CIU Medmenham, pored over the prints. The first print of the run over the airfield revealed the cruciform shape of a V-1 in position on a launching rail, while other prints in the sequence showed buildings of similar size and shape to those photographed in the Pas de Calais earlier that month. Quite by accident therefore, while searching for more information about German rocket development, Merifield's photographs had established beyond doubt that the imminent cross-channel threat was going to

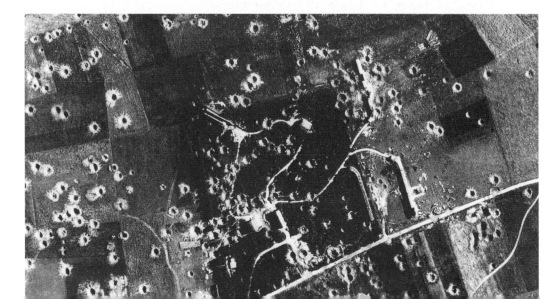

Above: A V-1 flying bomb, its wings detached, is craned onto a handling bogie before it is taken to the launching platform for assembly and launch.

Left: The so-called ski sites were very hard to spot from the air as this low-level oblique photograph shows. By November 10, 1943, a total of 26 ski sites had been found by photographic interpreters at CIU Medmenham.

*Below Left:*The ski-site at Bois Carré near Yvrench was the first to be found in November 1943. Extensive bombing of this and other ski sites in the Pas de Calais area was undertaken by heavy bombers of the USAAF on Christmas Eve 1943.

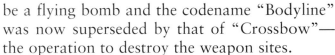

Above Left and Above: Once the V-1 flying bombs had come within range of British defences, more than one-tenth were shot down into the sea by fighters, and some by AA fire. Of the remainder that crossed the coast, more than half were brought down over land by fighters, AA fire, or balloon barrages. In this remarkable photograph taken by a USAAF F-5 on July 4, 1944, a flying bomb is pursued across the English countryside by a Hawker Tempest fighter aircraft.

be a flying bomb and the codename "Bodyline" was now superseded by that of "Crossbow"— the operation to destroy the weapon sites.

From the evidence available it became obvious that the ski sites had to be bombed, and soon, before they could launch their flying bombs at England. RAF Bomber Command mounted the first in a prolonged series of bombing raids against V-sites on December 16/17 when a mixed force of 47 aircraft, including nine Lancasters of No 617 Squadron, raided sites near Abbeville. The Stirlings of No 3 Group, which had recently been withdrawn from Main Force raids on Germany, were put to good use on these relatively lightly defended targets closer to home.

On Christmas Eve, 722 B-17s and B-24s of the US 8th Air Force's 1st, 2nd and 3rd Bomb Divisions launched a heavy raid on all the ski sites in the Pas de Calais with devastating results and the immediate threat from the V-1 was neutralised. Heavy bomber squadrons of RAF Bomber Command and the US 8th Air Force continued to mount attacks on V-sites in the Pas de Calais and Cherbourg areas by day and night whenever the weather or other considerations prevented attacks on Germany, and they continued to do so in the months leading up to D-Day and beyond. Medium bombers and fighter-bombers of the RAF's 2nd TAF and the US 9th Air Force added further weight to the attacks by day. When the Germans realized that effecting

repairs to the ski sites was a waste of time, they set about constructing a series of new and simpler launch sites.

A fresh cover of the Cherbourg peninsula flown in April 1944 revealed the first of the new simpler sites, well camouflaged and very hard to spot from the air. They comprised a concrete base for the launching ramp and a square building nearby, but nothing more. A special flying program of reconnaissance flights was laid on and. by the beginning of June, 68 modified sites had been found. Although they looked unfinished, a further cover of the training center at Zinnowitz provided vital clues that showed they could be made ready for use within 48 hours. In the days immediately after the Normandy landings on June 6, PR coverage of the V-sites was low on the list of priorities, but on the 11th special Crossbow sorties were flown and nine sites that had not been photographed since D-Day were covered. Late in the evening of the 11th, Kendall reviewed the prints and, realising immediately that the sites were ready for use, sent off the "Diver" signal to the Chiefs of Staff telling them that an attack should be expected imminently. The first V-1 flying bombs landed on Britain in the early hours of June 13, and in the worst incident a railway bridge was hit at Bethnal Green in east London, causing extensive damage, killing six and making 200 homeless. More were to follow, and thick and fast.

Between June and August 1944, the fighter-bomber, medium, and heavy bomber squadrons of the RAF and the USAAF did everything possible to knock out the dozens of small launching ramps hidden in the countryside of the Pas de Calais. On June 20, 137 B-17s of the US 8th Air Force's 3rd Bomb Division raided the V 1 assembly plant in the Volkswagenwerk at Fallersleben, repeated nine days later by a force of B-24s, with great success. Although bomber support for Allied troops breaking out from the Normandy beach-head was the priority, both air forces continued to fly thousands of largely successful sorties by day and night against flying bomb launch sites and storage installations, until at last in September most had been overrun and captured by advancing Allied troops. By the end of the month, 133 modified sites had been identified from the air by PR sorties over northern France. Only eight sites had defied identification by PR and they were so well camouflaged that only ground intelligence could have revealed them.

While most effort in the months that led up to D-Day had been directed towards solving the V-1 riddle, investigation into the other secret weapon, the V-2 rocket, had taken a back seat. But intelligence gathering continued and reports reaching London in March 1944 told of the Germans conducting rocket tests at a place called Blizna in southeast Poland. On April 15 an RAF Mosquito of the Mediterranean Allied PR Wing flew to Poland from its base at San Severo, near Foggia, in Italy, to photograph

Above Right: With the destruction of V-2 launching sites at Watten in August 1943, construction of an alternative bomb-proof site was begun at Wizernes nearby. Bombing attacks on the site commenced in March 1944 but construction continued until brought to a halt by the attack by RAF Bomber Command on July 17, using 12,000lb "Tallboy" deep penetration bombs. This oblique photograph was taken on a daring low-level sortie by a PR Mosquito several days before the "Tallboy" raid.

Right: The V-1 launching site at Domart-en-Ponthieu (Flixecourt) in the Somme, under attack on January 14, 1944 by Bostons of the RAF's 2nd Air Force.

Blizna, but the results it brought home were inconclusive. A second cover on May 5 caught a rocket in the open and revealed that it had four fins and was transported by a special trailer, evidence that linked in with intelligence reports from agents on the ground. The War Cabinet became concerned that a rocket offensive might be imminent and so Medmenham was called upon to provide some answers, and quickly.

Intensive PR of northern France in July 1943 had revealed large concrete emplacements under construction at Wissant near Cap Gris Nez, with a newly laid railway siding. By the end of the

Above and Below: The underground V-2 rocket factory at Nordhausen in the Harz mountains was captured by US forces in April 1945. They removed 100 completed rockets for shipment to America for test purposes. This V-2 was one of a train-load captured intact by the US First Army near Kassel in Germany.

month, three more had been identified close by at Naires Berne, Wambrigue, and Marquise. Their purpose was still not clear to the interpreters, but they were suspected of being connected with the German rocket program. During

the winter months of 1943-44 the sites were regularly photographed and bombed to hold up building progress.

Believing that the answers might lie in the re-interpretation of the previous covers of Peenemünde, Kendall re-examined thousands of prints from 35 sorties. His attention moved from the earthworks that characterized the site to a nearby stretch of foreshore. He concluded that an area of asphalt close to the sea with what appeared to be a thick column measuring some 40ft high was, in fact, a practice site for launching the V-2 rocket, and the 40ft column observed in the cover of June 1943 was a rocket standing on its fins. It was now clear that launch sites did not need to be served by a railway, and all that was needed to effect a launch was a road or clearing in a wood. The fact that the rocket launching apparatus was fully mobile by road, needed little in the way of fixed equipment, and could be moved with ease to new launch sites, were key factors in keeping it out of sight of prying cameras in PR aircraft.

The first V-2s were launched against England on September 8 from the Wassenaar district of The Hague in Holland, the first landing at 6.43pm in a residential street at Chiswick in west London where it blasted a huge crater and killed three people. For the reasons already described it proved impossible for PR aircraft to find the operational launching sites, but reports from agents on the ground pointed to The Hague and covers of the Haagsche Bosch in late December revealed that the central park was being used as a storage and launch area. Allied ground attacks on the Haagsche Bosch forced the Germans out and gave Londoners a short respite from attack by the V-2. They were soon resumed but this time, after seven months of fruitless searching, three PR Mosquitoes, operating indepedently of one another, struck it lucky on February 26 with chance sightings of a V-2 ready for launch with its fueling and support vehicles close by. The new launch area was pinpointed as Duindigt racecourse in the northeast suburbs of The Hague.

The attacks finally ceased on March 27, 1945, with the last V-2 to land in England falling at Orpington in Kent where it killed one person. A total of 1,115 rockets had been fired at London and southern England, killing 2,642 people in London and 213 elsewhere, before the remaining launch sites were captured by Allied troops.

As a sad postscript—and although unknown at the time—Bomber Command attacks on the German military barracks at Nordhausen on April 3 and 4 killed a number of concentration camp prisoners and other forced laborers who worked in a vast complex of underground tunnels building V-weapons.

Below: A V-2 rocket pictured alongside its launch apparatus at Peenemünde on May 23, 1944, ready for test-firing. It was captured on camera by a photo-reconnaissance aircraft of the RAF's No 544 Squadron.

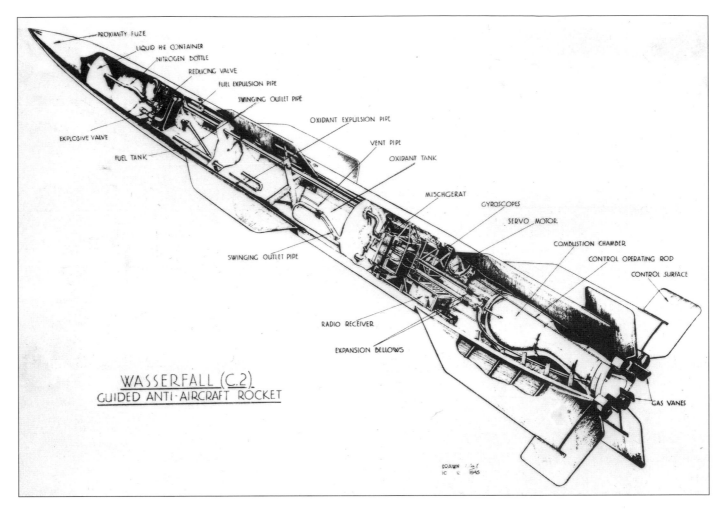

PROXIMITY FUZE
LIQUID H.E CONTAINER
NITROGEN BOTTLE
REDUCING VALVE
FUEL EXPULSION PIPE
SWINGING OUTLET PIPE
OXIDANT EXPULSION PIPE
VENT PIPE
OXIDANT TANK
EXPLOSIVE VALVE
FUEL TANK
MISCHGERAT
GYROSCOPES
SERVO MOTOR
COMBUSTION CHAMBER
CONTROL OPERATING ROD
CONTROL SURFACE
SWINGING OUTLET PIPE
RADIO RECEIVER
EXPANSION BELLOWS
GAS VANES

WASSERFALL (C.2)
GUIDED ANTI-AIRCRAFT ROCKET

DRAWN
10 2 1945

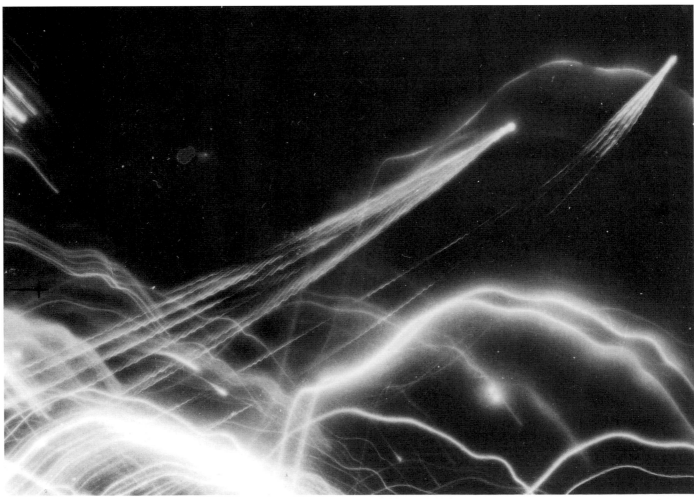

PERFORMANCE

The extensive PR sorties flown mainly by the RAF but with extensive support of the US 8th Air Force, were probably the most important contribution to the Allied war effort made by the PR squadrons. They provided visual proof of Hitler's V-weapons when confusion reigned in intelligence circles and gave vital information to the War Cabinet so they could coordinate civil defense measures. Without this intelligence there would have been little or no chance of discovering details of Hitler's secret weapons, and virtually no opportunity of countering them.

The information gleaned from reconnaissance photographs gave precise information about the locations of the dozens of V-sites and storage installations so that bombing attacks could be accurately targeted in the "Noball" campaign that followed D-Day.

Had it not been for the delay caused by heavy and accurate Allied bombing prior to D-Day, both the V-1 and V-2 would have become operational several months earlier and might have fatally disrupted preparations for the invasion of France and made the embarkation of troops and equipment almost impossible. As it was, by the time the Germans were ready to launch their flying bomb attack in mid-June 1944, the Allied armies had already landed on the coast of France and established secure bridgeheads in Normandy.

Unfortunately, PR had little success in finding the V-2 launch sites for the reasons already described, and therefore played little part in countering the rocket offensive once it had begun.

Above Left: Cutaway illustration of the Wasserfall guided anti-aircraft rocket, a scaled-down version of the V-2 with a range of about 30 miles—a precursor of the SAM missiles of the post-war period.

Left: Wasserfall AA rockets in action, their exhaust emissions leaving fiery trails in the night sky.

UNITS INVOLVED

RAF and USAAF PR units: Operations "Bodyline" and "Crossbow" 1942-1944.

1. RAF units
No 1 PRU Spitfire PR I, IV, Mosquito PR I, IV, Maryland I
(Disbanded October 1942 and reformed as Nos 540, 541, 542, 543, and 544 Squadrons)

No 540 Squadron Mosquito PR IV, VI, IX, XVI
Leuchars October 1942-February 1944; Benson February 1944-March 1945

No 541 Squadron Spitfire PR IV, VII, IX, X, XI, XIX, Mustang III
Benson October 1942-May 1945

No 542 Squadron Spitfire PR IV, VI, VII, IX, X, XI, XIX
Benson October 1942-May 1945

No 543 Squadron Spitfire PRIV, VII, IX
Benson October 1942-October 1943

No 544 Squadron Wellington VI, Anson I, Spitfire PR IV, XI, Maryland I, Mosquito PR IX, XVI
Benson October 1942-May 1945

No 682 Squadron Spitfire PR IV, XI, XIX, Mosquito PR IV, VI
San Severo, Italy, December 1943-September 1944

No 683 Squadron Spitfire PR IV, XI, XIX, Mosquito PR IV, VI
San Severo, Italy, December 1943-August 1945

2. USAAF UNITS
13th PR Squadron P-38, F-5
Mount Farm February 1943-December 1945

14th PR Squadron P-38, F-4, F-5, Spitfire
Mount Farm May 1943-December 1945

22nd PR Squadron (Light) P-38, Spitfire
Mount Farm June 1943-December 1945

27th PR Squadron P-38, F-4, F-5
Mount Farm November 1943-September 1944

OPERATION "MARKET GARDEN"

10 THE ADVANCE INTO HOLLAND, SEPTEMBER 1944

MISSION AIM

By September 1944 the Allies' astonishingly rapid progress through France and Belgium following the landings on the Normandy beaches in June was beginning to slow down. In an attempt to finish the war by Christmas, Montgomery, commander of the British 21st Army Group and who had been recently promoted to Field Marshal, persuaded the Supreme Allied Commander, Gen Eisenhower, to allow him to try to outflank the German defenses with a major thrust north through the Netherlands.

The plan was daring. The British Second Army under Gen M. Dempsey was to break out at the Belgian/Dutch border and dash to the Rhine crossing at Arnhem on the German/Dutch border. Three airborne divisions of the First Allied Airborne Army were to be dropped to capture vital river and canal crossings along the route, holding them until relieved by the Second Army, spearheaded by XXXth Corps under Lt-Gen B. Horrocks, which was to reach Arnhem in

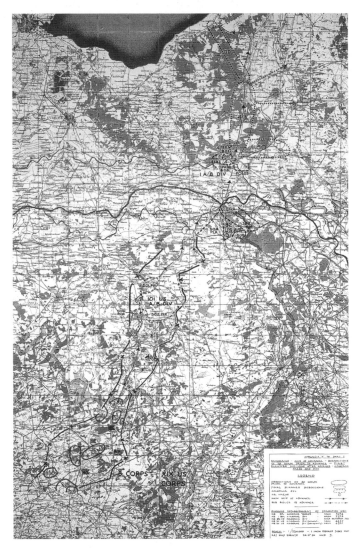

Above: Map showing the plan for Operation "Market Garden." It was intended that XXXth Corps was to relieve the three Allied drop areas of Eindhoven, Nijmegen, and Arnhem in two days, opening the way into Germany.

Left: Reconnaissance photograph of the town of Arnhem taken a few days before the operation, showing the objective of the road bridge over the Rhine and the open ground to the south of the river.

two days. At that time this was the largest Allied airborne operation of the war but only one week was given for First Allied Airborne to plan and mount the operation, and many of the seeds for the ultimate failure of the operation, code-named "Market Garden," were sown in the planning.

BACKGROUND

In command of the First Allied Airborne Army was Lt-Gen L. H. Brereton but his deputy Lt-Gen F. M. "Boy" Browning took command of the three divisions of First Allied Airborne for the operation. The US 101st Airborne Division was to capture the bridges between Eindhoven and Grave, the US 82nd Airborne Division was to take the crossings between Grave and Nijmegen, and the British 1st Airborne Division, aided by the 1st Polish Independent Parachute Brigade, was to capture the road and rail bridges across the Rhine at Arnhem.

One of the main logistical problems confronting the planners was that there were not enough aircraft to get all of the three divisions to their destinations in one lift. The vital element of surprise, usually the key to success for comparatively lightly armed airborne troops, in this case would be lost, allowing the Germans time to regroup and counter-attack. In fact, there were only enough aircraft to lift about a third of the troops at a time, the remainder would have to be delivered piecemeal over the two days following the initial drops. The timescale for the drops was further extended because night flying was rejected due to the USAAF's lack of experience and fear of serious navigational errors.

The choice of drop zones (DZ) and landing zones (LZ) was another problem for the planners to resolve. With the exception of the bridge at Nijmegen, the objectives of the US 101st and 82nd were lightly defended by flak and they were able to land near them. Intelligence reports of heavy anti-aircraft defenses around the town of Arnhem and PR evidence that the ground immediately to the south of the river was unsuitable for landings, being swampy and criss-crossed with dykes, meant that the commander of 1st Airborne Division, Maj-Gen R. E. Urquhart, reluctantly agreed to DZs and LZs on open ground about seven miles west of Arnhem, near the suburb Oosterbeek. The ensuing delay in reaching the bridges at Arnhem was to prove another factor in the failure of "Market Garden." Furthermore, PR by the Spitfire XIs, Mosquitoes and Mustangs of No 35 (Recce) Wing of No 84 Group and No 39 (Recce) Wing of No 83 Group of the RAF in the week leading up to the drop had been patchy due to other commitments (including the search for V-2 launching sites) and frequent poor visibility meant that little conclusive evidence of enemy movements emerged. Intelligence had received some reports from the Dutch Resistance of an enemy build-up in the Arnhem area and a low-level sortie by the RAF produced a few photographs showing tanks that were shown to Lt-Gen Browning, but these were not taken seriously. In fact, the heavily wooded area around Arnhem was sheltering the 2nd SS Panzer Corps, comprising 9th and 10th SS Divisions and the 1st Airborne Division was to walk straight into them.

THE COURSE OF THE BATTLE

D-Day was Sunday, September 17, 1944. As the armada of C-47 transport aircraft, tugs, gliders (the Americans using Wacos and the British using Horsas and Hamilcar cargo gliders) and fighter escort left England in two groups, one flying over the North Sea, the other crossing the Channel, the RAF was carrying out armed reconnaissance over the LZs and DZs. From the previous night onwards the RAF and USAAF had also bombed enemy defenses in the objective areas. Pathfinders landed first and guided the rest of the aircraft in with radio beacons, marker panels and smoke signals.

At 13.00hrs the US 101st Airborne Diision, under the command of Maj-Gen M. Taylor, began its drop of 6,809 paratroops.

Flak was heavy but casualties were low and within an hour all the units had regrouped and begun to move off towards their objectives. By 15.00hrs the bridges over the Aa and the Zuid Willemsvaart Canal had been seized by the 501st Parachute Infantry Regiment, commanded by Col Howard R. Johnston. At nightfall the town of Veghel was reached in spite of resistance from small enemy units, the bridges were secured, and the troops dug in.

The landing of the 502nd Parachute Infantry Regiment, under the command of Col J. H. Michaelis, was trouble-free. After a skirmish the town of St Oedenrode was taken by the 1st Battalion, securing their objective of the bridge

over the Dommet, but it was at the road bridge at Best that the first real resistance was encountered at a German roadblock. The 3rd Battalion had got lost on the way, only one platoon initially reaching the bridge, and it was not until the next morning that the rest of the battalion arrived and the bridge could be taken.

At DZ "C" the 506th Parachute Infantry Regiment also managed to land without opposition. Its objective was to seize three bridges over the Wilhelmina Canal and it got to within 100yd of the the main bridge at Zon before it was blown up. The other bridges were likewise destroyed by the Germans but nonetheless, by the end of the day, the regiment had managed to get across the canal.

In the Nijmegen area Brig-Gen J. Gavin's 82nd US Airborne Division encountered heavy flak over the DZs and LZs but losses were slight. The first paratroops were dropped at 12.50hrs and the gliders landed one hour later. The first

Above Left: The tugs and gliders on their way to Arnhem.

Left: Horsa and Hamilcar gliders scattered thickly on the ground on their LZ at Arnhem.

Below: US 101st Airborne Division assault area.

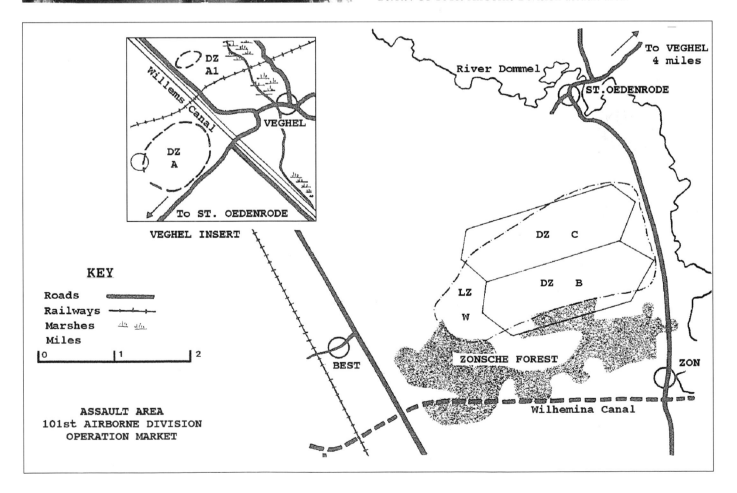

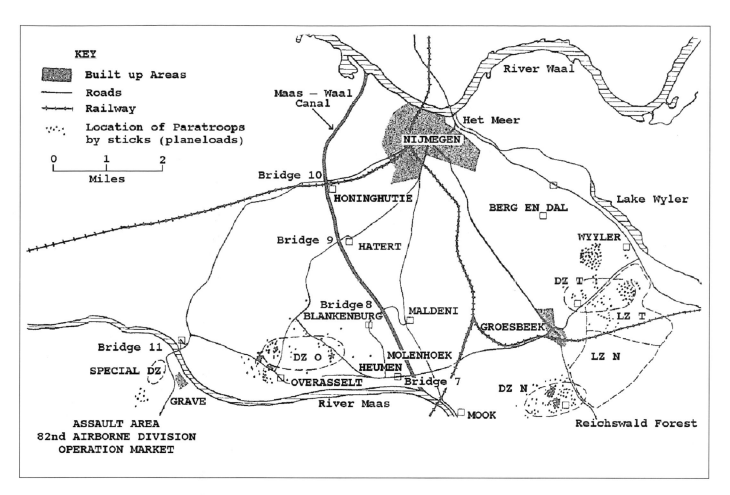

KEY

▨ Built up Areas
⊢⊣ Roads
⊢┼┼┼⊣ Railway
⋰⋱ Location of Paratroops
by sticks (planeloads)

0   1   2
Miles

River Waal

Maas – Waal Canal

NIJMEGEN

Het Meer

Bridge 10

HONINGHUTIE

BERG EN DAL

Lake Wyler

Bridge 9

HATERT

WYYLER

DZ T

LZ T

Bridge 8
BLANKENBURG

MALDENI

GROESBEEK

LZ N

Bridge 11

DZ O

MOLENHOEK

SPECIAL DZ

HEUMEN

Bridge 7

OVERASSELT

River Maas

DZ N

GRAVE

MOOK

Reichswald Forest

ASSAULT AREA
82nd AIRBORNE DIVISION
OPERATION MARKET

Above: US 82nd Airborne Division assault area.

Left: US Waco gliders marshaled prior to take-off from their troop carrier base in England.

Below Left: Most of the aircraft of the vast air armada reached their objectives but there were inevitably some casualties on the way. Here a US glider is being rescued by a launch, having being forced to ditch in the North Sea.

objective was the Groesbeek Heights, an area of high ground southeast of Nijmegen, which was quickly seized by the 505th Parachute Infantry Regiment. To the west of the Maas-Waal Canal was the DZ of the 504th Parachute Infantry Regiment, commanded by Col R. H. Tucker. Here the German resistance was stiffer and the first bridge over the canal was captured only after two hours of fierce fighting. The Germans had managed to blow up other bridges over the canal at Blankenburg and Hatert but both sites were captured that night. The main road bridge over the Maas at Grave had also been seized at 14.30hrs and by the end of the day the regiment was occupying the town of Grave, having forced the Germans to withdraw.

The final objective was the vitally important 1,960ft-long road bridge over the River Waal at Nijmegen. The 508th Parachute Infantry Regiment had been dropped northeast of

Groesbeek and after the area was secured the 1st Battalion was ordered to move on to capture the bridge. In spite of the large number of German troops in the area, the paratroops managed to penetrate the town to within 400yd of the bridge before they met stiff resistance which halted them. However, although the bridge was not captured, the Germans were prevented from blowing it up.

1st Airborne Division's drop over Arnhem was also achieved with few losses in spite of the flak and the majority of the gliders landed unscathed. By 15.00hrs the troops had regrouped and were in position to move off toward their objectives. The 1st Air-Landing Brigade's job was to protect the LZs and DZs for

Above: US paratroops receiving last minute instructions from the jump-master just before take-off. Unlike the British each had a reserve parachute, seen strapped to their fronts.

Right: USAAF Douglas C-47s carrying paratroops en route to Holland.

Below Right: The crowded sky of a paratroop drop, taken by an observer with a camera strapped to his chest during the 4th Parachute Brigade's drop in the second lift to Arnhem.

Bottom Right: Additional paratroops of the US 82nd Airborne Division being dropped on D+2 near Grave. In the foreground can be seen the Waco gliders which arrived on D-Day.

training battalion that had been carrying out exercises in the area and had seen the drop, and was forced to withdraw at 18.30hrs. Communications problems at this stage were begining to mount as the radios could not operate effectively in the heavily wooded area and the 2nd Battalion, unaware of the disarray, pressed on towards Arnhem. At the same time, due to the breakdown in radio communications, Urquhart and Lathbury set off from HQ after them to urge troops on the southern route to move as fast as possible in an attempt to salvage the operation.

Despite some skirmishes around Oosterbeek 2nd Battalion under the command of Lt-Col J. Frost reached Arnhem. The railway bridge had earlier been blown up by the Germans just as a platoon of 2nd Battalion had reached it, but at 20.00hrs, after sporadic fighting along the approach road, the road bridge was reached by A Company. Advancing onto the bridge, several times they were thrown back by fire from the defenders' bunkers, and forced to consolidate their position on the north end of the bridge and

the second lift the following day; the task of the 1st Parachute Brigade, under the command of Brig G. Lathbury, was to take the bridge at Arnhem. The 1st Airborne Reconnaissance Squadron led by Maj C. F. H. Gough was to rush to the bridge using armoured jeeps in a *coup de main* assault, three battalions of the 1st Parachute Brigade were to head for Arnhem on foot: 2nd Parachute Battalion taking the southern route along the river, 3rd Parachute Battalion heading southeast to take the main road to Arnhem, and 1st Parachute Battalion, in reserve, to enter Arnhem from the north.

Gough was soon held up by fierce German resistance in the town of Wolfheze from a SS

Below: The DZs and LZs of the British 1st Airborne Division at Arnhem, showing also the final divisional perimeter around Oosterbeek.

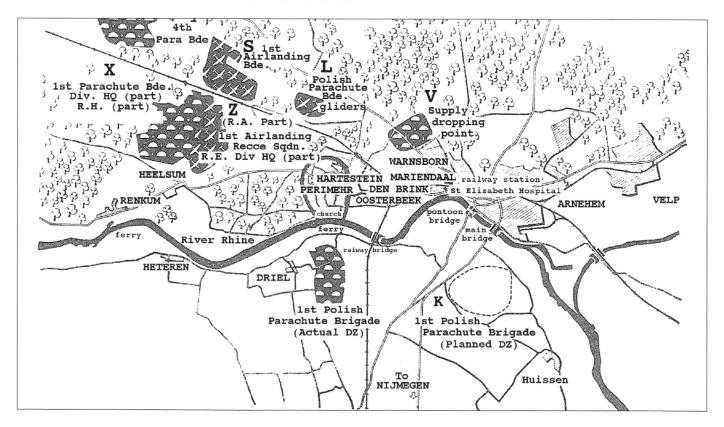

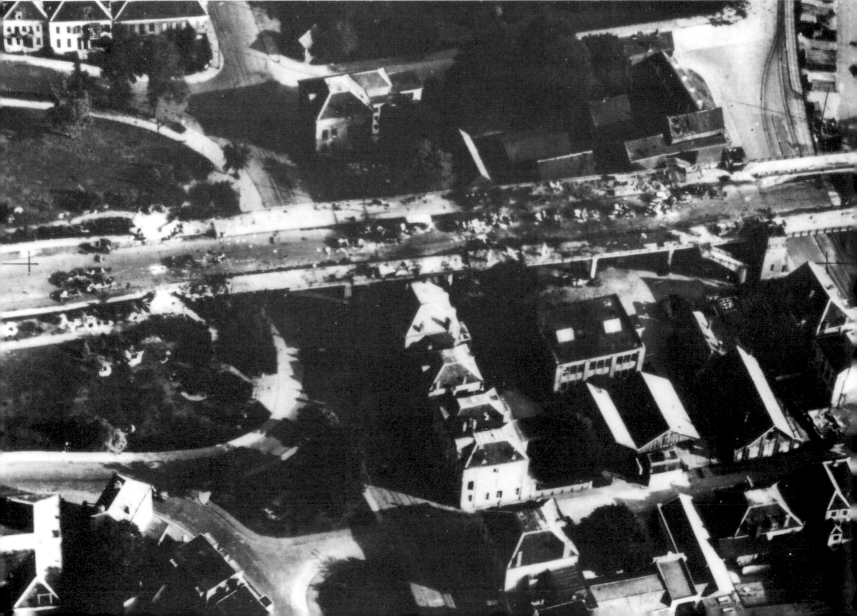

Above Left: 1st Airborne Division's parachutes blossom from the low-flying Dakotas over the DZ at Arnhem.

Below Left: A low-level reconnaissance photograph taken by a PRU Spitfire showing the destroyed enemy armor on the road bridge at Arnhem after Col Frost's 2nd Parachute Battalion had repulsed the attack of the 9th SS Panzer Division's reconnaissance unit early in the morning of September 18.

in the surrounding buildings. As time passed, German reinforcements moved towards the area from the north and south and became involved in heavy fighting at the bridge which gradually died down during the night. As 2nd Battalion settled down to await reinforcements they were not to know that none of the the other battalions were able to reach them because of the strength of German defenses in the area.

While the three drops were taking place the XXXth Corps launched its attack, smashing through German defenses to the south. Once on the road to Eindhoven, the problems of the terrain in the area (which were to prove another fatal factor in the operation's eventual failure) soon became apparent. As the ground beside the road was marshy, the road quickly became jammed with tanks, held up by a series of ambushes. These German anti-tank guns were eventually destroyed by the British armor supported by Typhoon fighter-bombers but by 19.30hrs the corps had only reached Valkenswaard, where it halted, indicative of the painfully slow progress it was to make over the next few days. It did not move on again until the next day, when it continued towards Eindhoven.

Around Eindhoven on September 18, 1944—D+1 — the US 501st Parachute Infantry Regiment continued to hold Veghel and St Oedenrode. It suffered heavy casualties in the attempt to take the road bridge at Best, which the Germans succeeded in blowing up.

At dawn the 506th, led by the 3rd Battalion, began to advance on Eindhoven. A mile outside the town they were held up by determined resistance but the 2nd Battalion managed to outflank the defenses and the town was taken at 13.00hrs. Around midafternoon, gliders brought in 3rd Battalion, 327th Glider Infantry Regiment as well as an engineer battalion, signals, and much needed artillery and medical supplies.

Later that day at 19.15hrs the leading element of the XXXth Corps, the Guards Armoured Division, linked up with the 506th south of the town. They were already behind schedule and during the night worked to build a bridge across

the Wilhelmina Canal so that they could move off again at daybreak.

To the north the 504th was holding the bridges over the Maas-Waal Canal and the Maas at Grave. The Grave-Nijmegen road was kept open by patrols, despite a bridge near Honinghutie being destroyed by the Germans, and after withdrawing at the start of the day, the town of Nijmegen was taken by the 508th. In the 505th's area near Groesbeek four German battle groups counter-attacked at 06.30hrs. The 505th was stretched for a time in the fierce fighting which threatened the DZs and LZs which were awaiting the second drop scheduled for 13.00hrs. Gradually, the attacks were beaten off but sporadic fighting was still going on when the gliders landed late at 14.30hrs.

At Arnhem on D+1, 1st British Airborne Division was without its leader as Urquhart and Lathbury, after having reached 3rd Battalion, had become trapped in Arnhem, unable to get back to HQ at Oosterbeek. Acting commander Brig Hicks ordered Brig J. W. Hackett, who had come in with the drop that day of 4th Parachute Brigade, to send the 11th Parachute Battalion to support the exhausted 2nd Battalion at the bridge, where the 9th SS Panzer Division Reconnaissance Company had been knocked back as they attempted to cross the bridge at dawn. The 4th Parachute Brigade was to capture the high ground to the north of the town but for the rest of this and the next day it fought in vain, suffering heavy casualties.

At 10.00hrs on D+2 the XXXth Corps' Guards Armoured Division crossed the bridge at Grave to link up with the 504th and 505th Regiments in the 82nd's area. Earlier that day the XXXth Corps had moved through Vegel and St Oedenrode and, despite German resistance, the bridges at Best and Zon had been secured by the end of the day, reinforced by the 101st's third drop in the afternoon of further infantry and artillery. The next main objectives for the combined force of the Guards Armoured Division, Grenadier Guards, and the US 505th Regiment were the road and rail bridges at Nijmegen, which were defended by the 10th SS Panzer Division. The strength of the German defenses and the heavy casualties suffered by the combined force at the bridges meant that the advance stalled yet again short of its objective.

According to the original plan the 1st British Airborne Division should have had to wait only two days before being relieved by the advancing armor but as September 19 wore on, the troops at Arnhem and Oosterbeek became increasingly entrapped. Urquhart had managed to get back early that morning and, in the face of the worsening situation, decided that he had to order 4th Parachute Brigade to withdraw to defend the divisional perimeter at Oosterbeek. This meant that the remnants of 2nd Parachute Battalion would be abandoned to their fate at the bridge at Arnhem. D+2 was when the 1st Polish Parachute Brigade, commanded by Maj-Gen S. Sosabowski, was due to arrive, but fog over England meant only the gliders arrived. The Polish landing zone was to south of the bridge at Arnhem, across the river from the 1st Airborne Division. Heavy flak and fierce fighting on the ground when they landed, just as 4th Parachute Brigade was retreating, meant that the Poles suffered heavy casualties, the survivors joining the withdrawal towards Oosterbeek.

The 2nd Parachute Battalion managed to cling on at the bridge for another day, finally being overrun by the Germans when they ran out of ammunition shortly after dawn on September 21. The rest of the troops at Oosterbeek were being worn down by the constant German shelling and mortaring as well as

infantry, self-propelled weapons and tank attacks. XXXth Corps was again moving slowly, held up by 10th SS Panzer Division, but a brave river crossing under fire by the 3rd Battalion of the US 504th Parachute Infantry Regiment meant that the Guards Armoured Division could cross the Waal in the afternoon, although the advance soon halted again.

The Polish paratroopers finally arrived at Arnhem on D+4, September 21, but could not get across the river to join the troops who were on their last legs as the trap was closing at Oosterbeek. Sosabowski had no option then but to dig in and await XXXth Corps, who finally linked up with them late the next day. During the night of September 22/23 an attempt to get the Poles across failed, only 50 making it to the other side of the river. Two nights later a further attempt to get the 4th Battalion Dorsetshire Regiment across also failed, only about half of them making it.

It was not until six days after the first drop that the decision was finally taken to evacuate 1st Airborne Division. The attempt to keep the 60-mile corridor from Eindhoven and Nijmegen towards Arnhem open had proved costly for the US 82nd and 101st Airborne Divisions, as they had been subjected to frequent German counterattacks attempting to sever the highway and it was becoming clear that XXXth Corps would not be able to get through fully to establish a permanent bridgehead across the Rhine.

Below: A mortar crew of the 1st Battalion, The Border Regiment, in action during the increasingly desperate defence of the perimeter at Oosterbeek.

Left: Casualties among all ranks were heavy for both sides. Gen Kussin, the German area commander at Arnhem, was ambushed and killed in his staff car by 3rd Parachute Battalion whilst on the road between Arnhem and Oosterbeek.

On the night of September 25/26, while diversionary firing by the few remaining troops plus a heavy artillery bombardment by XXXth Corps distracted the Germans, giving the impression of fierce fighting, Urquhart moved what was left of his division to a crossing point of the river. The evacuation lasted all night and by daybreak the last exhausted troops were across, moving to safety in Nijmegen later that day. Of the 10,005 who had landed, the 1st Airborne Division managed to get out only 2,163 men. Furthermore, over the course of the battle, the US 82nd Airborne had lost 1,432 men killed, missing, or wounded and the US 101st Airborne lost 1,652. The attempt to achive a quick finish to the war had been a costly failure.

PERFORMANCE

There were many reasons for this failure. Poor communications, not least between the tactical reconnaissance aircraft during the battle and the various ground battle areas, continually dogged the Allied advance and at Arnhem little use was made of the potential air power at their disposal to keep the airspace open for later drops and supplies, as well as attacking the German forces on the ground. The inability to take the bridges at Arnhem was crucial. The choice of drop zones several miles away from the bridges meant that the important element of surprise was lost, this was compounded by the fact that the drops took place in three stages allowing the Germans time to defend what were obviously the Allied objectives and then counter-attack. Night-drops may have helped as it would have meant that the numbers of Allied troops would have reached full force sooner. Taking the HQ to the Netherlands had diverted aircraft from carrying additional front-line troops.

It could also be argued that the RAF's PR had not been effective enough, leading it to over-estimate the strength of German anti-aircraft defenses at Arnhem and not risk a drop nearer the bridges, but the RAF's losses over Arnhem were proportionally as high as that of the troops on the ground. All of this was compounded by the slow progress of XXXth Corps along the corridor created by the US 82nd and 101st towards Arnhem allowing the Germans to bring in reinforcements. Overall, the Allies had underestimated the powers of recovery of the Wehrmacht after its retreat from Normandy. Vital clues to the ability of the German Army to regroup to defend the national borders, such as the indications from PR missions prior to the operation of significant armored strength in the area, had been ignored in the general desire to finish the war quickly. The failure of "Market Garden" was to mean that the war would drag on in to the next year.

OPERATION "VARSITY"

11 THE RHINE CROSSING, MARCH 24, 1945

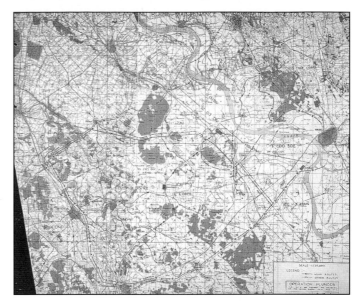

MISSION AIM

By January 1945 the last desperate German throw of the Ardennes offensive, begun in December 1944, had been contained. Two months later the Allies had reached the Rhine and were ready for a final push into Germany to finish the war. The front comprised three army groups: Field Marshal Montgomery's 21st was the northernmost, Brig-Gen O. Bradley's 12th was in the center and Maj-Gen J. Devers' 6th in the south. Montgomery was opposed by Gen J. Blaskowitz's Army Group H in north, defending the Ruhr.

Montgomery had arrived at the Rhine in February, building up his forces (the Canadian First, British Second, and US Ninth Armies) slowly on the west bank. He wanted to cross the river between Wesel and Emmerich in strength, as he anticipated tough opposition from the German 1st Parachute Army commanded by Gen Schlemm, and secure a bridgehead from

which his armored and infantry divisions could break out into north Germany. Gen Simpson's Ninth Army and Gen Dempsey's Second Army were to cross at the same time on March 24 with Dempsey's amphibious crossing being backed up by a daylight airborne drop to reinforce the bridgehead as quickly as possible.

The airborne drop was named Operation "Varsity." Unlike Arnhem, it was to provide weight to an already existing bridgehead and would be within the range of supporting artillery

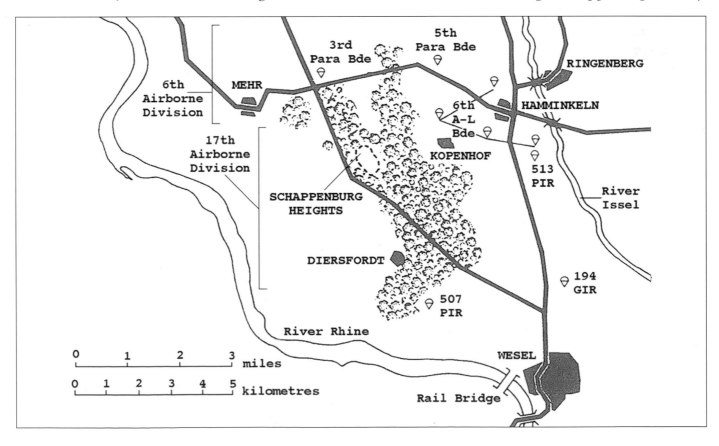

ALLIED PHOTO RECONNAISSANCE

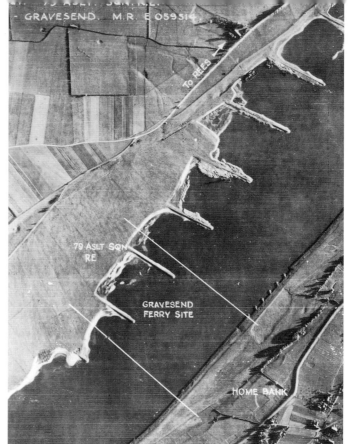

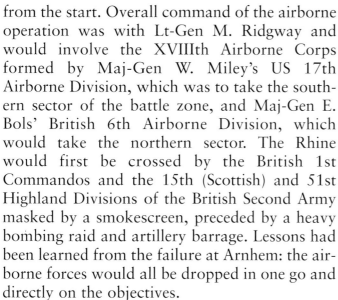

from the start. Overall command of the airborne operation was with Lt-Gen M. Ridgway and would involve the XVIIIth Airborne Corps formed by Maj-Gen W. Miley's US 17th Airborne Division, which was to take the southern sector of the battle zone, and Maj-Gen E. Bols' British 6th Airborne Division, which would take the northern sector. The Rhine would first be crossed by the British 1st Commandos and the 15th (Scottish) and 51st Highland Divisions of the British Second Army masked by a smokescreen, preceded by a heavy bombing raid and artillery barrage. Lessons had been learned from the failure at Arnhem: the airborne forces would all be dropped in one go and directly on the objectives.

The plan was for the airborne forces to seize the high ground of the Diersfordter Wald overlooking the crossing point after the Second Army had taken the town of Wesel. The airborne forces were then to take the road and rail bridges over the River Issel at the town of Hamminkeln—eight miles northeast of the bridgehead—to prevent reinforcing German troops attacking the crossing points. Detailed photographs of the drop zones supplied by aerial reconnaissance provided vital information in planning the drop, and the PR also indicated accurately German troop defenses and gun positions in the area, as well as the build-up of the numbers of enemy troops in the weeks before "Varsit." The Allies were forewarned that the Germans were preparing for an airborne assault.

Far Left: XIIth Corps map of the planned invasion of Germany (codenamed Operation "Plunder"), showing the intended crossing points on the Rhine for the British 2nd Army (including XIIth Corps) and the 9th US Army. Once across they were to link up with the bridgehead established north of Wesel by the XVIIIrd Airborne Corps comprising the 17th US Airborne Division and the British 6th Airborne Division.

Above Left and Above: Reconnaissance photographs showing the northernmost Rhine crossing points, assigned to XXXth Corps at Rees [*Above Left*] and nearby Gravesend [*Above*].

Bottom Left: DZs for Operation "Varsity."

Below: The airborne forces arrived in waves over Wesel. Xanten, on the western bank of the Rhine, is in the background.

THE COURSE OF THE BATTLE

During the night of March 23/24, Allied artillery started a fierce bombardment of German defenses across the Rhine, climaxing three days of heavy bombing and armed fighter-reconnaissance attacks on enemy movements, flak, and troop positions east of the Rhine. Nearly all of the bombing targets were successfully hit and USAAF and RAF fighters kept the skies clear of the Luftwaffe—the only disappointment being that the German flak batteries in the landing zones had been obscured by haze and only about half of them could be attacked.

At 21.00hrs that night the 1st Commando Brigade crossed the Rhine in its assault craft, and Wesel was attacked by RAF Lancaster bombers. At 22.00hrs XIIth Corps begun crossing near Xanten and an hour later XXXth Corps crossed to the north. At 04.00hrs next morning the US Ninth Army begun its crossing south of Wesel. By dawn several small bridgeheads were established on the east bank of the Rhine.

In England the British 6th Airborne Division began taking-off from its airfields at 07.30hrs that morning in its C-47 Dakotas, the tug aircraft and Horsa and Hamilcar gliders having taken off an hour earlier. They rendezvoused over Belgium with the C-47s, Curtiss C-46 Commandos, and gliders carrying the US 17th Airborne Division that had left its airfields around Paris at around the same time. A total of 21,680 troops were being carried by Nos 38 and 46 Groups RAF and IXth Troop Carrier Command USAAF.

The massive artillery bombardment on the German anti-aircraft defenses and the DZs themselves fell silent as the first paratroops came in at 10.00hrs. As the enemy recovered from the barrage, anti-aircraft fire intensified at the aircraft which presented easy targets as they ran in straight, low and slow over the DZs.

Col E. Raff, commanding officer of the US 507th Parachute Infantry Regiment, was first out for his regiment. The intense flak meant that the majority of the regiment were dropped away from the objective of the heights around Diersfordter castle and in the first hour had to knock out the enemy machine guns and artillery, including a battery of 150mm guns, in the Diersfordter woods before they could regroup but by 11.00hrs the Diersfordter village had been taken along with 340 German prisoners.

The 2nd Battalion of the 507th, however, was dropped in the correct position, landing in a hail of rifle and machine gun fire from the village of Flüren and nearby woods. They managed to clear the woods within the hour, with the help of the 464th Parachute Field Artillery and its machine guns and howitzers, which had also landed on the DZ, and by 14.30hrs had made contact with the right flank of the ground troops advancing from the Rhine.

Below Left: Ground troops started the Rhine crossing in their assault craft during the night of March 23/24. An LVT is shown leaving the western bank.

Below: Tank wading screens being inflated prior to the Rhine crossing. In the foreground are the used compressed-air cylinders.

Left: Heavily laden with troops, an LVT makes its way towards German territory on the far bank of the river. Further Allied ground troops are ahead.

Below: At dawn on March 24 British troops embark in storm boats to cross the Rhine.

The 3rd Battalion, meanwhile, had advanced towards the castle as soon as the village had been taken. There the fighting lasted until early afternoon and seven tanks issuing from the castle had to be destroyed but by 14.58hrs Col Raff could report that the castle, and all the other objectives of the 507th, had been captured, along with 1,000 prisoners.

Commanded by Col J. Coutts, the US 513th Parachute Infantry Regiment's landing, planned for an area of fields on the east side of the Diersfordter Wald near the railway line from Wesel, was less successful. They had been using new, faster Curtiss C-46s, which could carry more men than the C-47 and had doors either side of the fuselage to enable the paratroops to be dropped faster, but a design fault with the fuel tanks which were not self-sealing meant that, in the heavy enemy fire over the landing zone, around 20 of them were shot down in flames, and many others were badly damaged. Nonetheless, many of the paratroops managed to jump only to find that, due to the smoke and dust covering the battlefield, they had been mistakenly dropped on the British 6th Air-Landing Brigade's LZ near the town of Hamminkeln, two miles from their own DZ. They landed in the middle of German defenses and many were killed before they had even struggled free of their parachutes, attempting at the same time to get out of the way of the 6th's descending gliders. However, their prompt attack on the German positions drew some of the fire away from the gliders, otherwise the 6th would have suffered heavier losses.

The first task of 2nd Battalion was to clear the enemy from all the farms and woods in the area. One farm, Kopenhof farm, was the scene of particularly desperate German defense, the first attack being repulsed by machine gun fire with heavy losses, and it took a brave and ultimately fatal charge straight at the farm by Pte Stryker before the farm was taken. Soon after, the edge of Diersfordter Wald was reached and the gap between the 507th Regiment and the British 3rd Para Brigade had been filled, contact actually being made with the British 9th Para Battalion.

In the confusion of the drop, 3rd Battalion had set off in what was thought to be the direction of their objective, the River Issel, only to discover they were nearing Hamminkeln. However, they changed direction and made up for the lost time; by 16.00hrs they were holding the river with the Royal Ulster Rifles and 194th Glider Infantry.

Col J. Pierce's 194th Glider Infantry Regiment, accompanied by the 466th Parachute Artillery, plus engineers, signals, and support

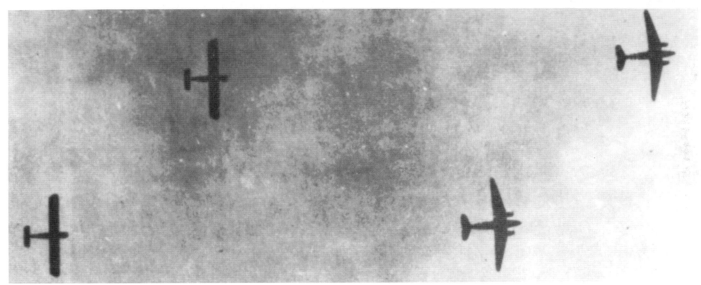

Top: A parachute column of C-47s heading towards the DZ in nine-ship elements made up of groups of three aircraft in V-formation.

Above: A pair of gliders with tugs, flying in echelon.

troops did manage to find the correct target in their Wacos but, landing in the middle of German flak and field artillery positions, they were without the help of any of their parachute infantry battalions. It was some time before they could overcome the opposition in the chaos of the landing—virtually every glider had been hit and 100 of the 570 gliders had crash-landed— but by noon they had cleared the enemy from the landing zone. They could then move towards securing their position along the bank of the Issel canal and the bridges over the River Issel, knocking out 10 German tanks and 42 guns in the course of the fighting and swelling their total of prisoners to 1,150. By 12.30hrs they were dug in, easily managing to beat back three German counter-attacks later that day.

The operation was going just as well in the British 6th Airborne Division's sector. The 3rd Para Brigade, including its commanding officer Brig J. Hill, had a near perfect drop on the northern side of the Diersfordter Wald. The 8th Parachute Battalion was first in. It went straight into action and cleared the drop zone quickly after some hard fighting against some German 7th *Fallschirmjäger* Division defenses in the nearby woods, which at first beat back B Company, killing their CO, Maj J. Kippin. 3rd Para was followed in by the 1st Canadian Parachute Battalion who came under heavy fire as they landed, losing several men during the drop and more when they became tangled in the trees. Amongst them was the CO, Lt-Col J. Nicklin, who landed in a tree above a machine gun position. Again, however, once the men were down the nearest enemy gun crews were quickly put out of action. In the houses along the road the *Fallschirmjäger* continued to fight doggedly, mortaring and machine-gunning the Canadian positions, but after a couple of hours these last ditch defenses were also overcome.

Last to jump was the 9th Parachute Battalion, led by Lt-Col N. Crookenden, only meeting light resistance as it landed and moving quickly off to clear the enemy batteries from the Schnappenburg heights, from where they had been firing on 15th Scottish Division advancing from the Rhine. By 13.00hrs they were dug into their final positions, linking up with the US 513th later that afternoon.

The three battalions of the 5th Para Brigade, commanded by Brig N. Poett, encountered heavy German fire when they landed just after 10.00hrs west of the Diersfordter Wald. Initially, the 7th and 12th Parachute Battalions were pinned down by heavy machine gun, mortar, and artillery fire, while attempting to regroup in the disorientating haze. A particularly troublesome battery of 88mm guns had to be taken out with a bayonet charge but, despite suffering heavy casualties, as soon as they had regrouped they moved off to take their objectives. some nearby buildings and a farm. By the time that the 13th Parachute Battalion had landed, the entire area was covered in dust and smoke but by virtue of the unusual rallying device of their commanding officers' hunting horns, they regrouped quickly and went straight into action.

After the initial intense combat the fighting gradually quietened and by 15.00hrs the brigade had secured all its objectives. They had secured the ground on either side of the road to Hammenkiln, and a nearby rail junction—defended by a platoon of 7th Battalion in the face of repeated attacks from the German 7th *Fallschirmjäger* Division. The gap between the 3rd and 5th Brigade had been closed and contact been made with the ground forces.

When planning this operation it was realized that speed would be a vital factor in its success. The British paratroops jumped in a sequence which related to the positions they had to take up on the ground and superfluous items of equipment were discarded so that troops could go straight into action as soon as they hit the ground. The paratroops at "Varsity" had generally landed in tight order and it was the glider landings following that had taken the brunt of enemy fire and suffered more chaos on landing.

The 6th Air-Landing Brigade had problems finding the LZ due to the smoke and dust, and the German anti-aircraft defenses had had longer to recover from the preliminary barrage by the time the gliders came in. Several gliders and their tugs were hit and 10 gliders were shot down with heavy losses of men. There were further casualties on the ground as many gliders collided due to the poor visibility, 32 being destroyed, but 90 percent of the Horsas and Hamilcars managed to land successfully. Again, the haze meant that they had been dropped slightly off target, the British practice being to release the gliders at 2,500ft over the target area (the Americans' preferred height being, by contrast, 600ft).

Enough of the 12th Devonshires, 2nd Oxfordshire and Buckinghamshire Light Infantry, and 1st Royal Ulster Rifles managed to land safely, and with the help of the US 513th Parachute Infantry, who had been mistakenly dropped on the glider LZ, the 12th Devonshires and 1st Royal Ulster Rifles managed to capture Hamminkeln, including the railway station. The 2nd "Ox and Bucks" took the bridges over the River Issel and by midday they were dug in. Later that night they were attacked over the

Below: Late in the afternoon of March 24 DUKWs began ferrying supplies of ammunition, medical stores, food, and petrol to the two airborne divisions across the river.

road bridge by German infantry and tanks, forcing them to blow up the bridge.

The problems of the glider landing meant that a large number of the vehicles, artillery, light tanks, and ammunition for the operation were lost. Fortunately the close artillery support from the other side of the river and the swift link-up with the ground troops meant that these losses did not prove serious. At 17.00hrs the DUKW amphibious trucks were able to cross the Rhine safely with further supplies, ferrying back the wounded.

Air reconnaissance during the battle had also been vital—by midday American L-19 and British Auster observation light aircraft were flying over both airborne divisions, helping provide the communications links and information that were vital to the artillery west of the Rhine and on the battlefield. Air power was driven home when 240 USAAF B-24 bombers followed the last troop aircraft loaded with supplies for the two airborne divisions which they managed to drop successfully on the battlefield. These too suffered heavy casualties that day—15 of them were shot down immediately afterwards before they could turn back over the Rhine.

At the end of the day Maj-Gen Ridgway and Maj-Gen Miley joined Maj-Gen Bols at the HQ of 6th Airborne Division, the two Americans undeterred by an earlier encounter with a group of German soldiers in which Ridgway suffered a slight wound from a grenade exploding in his jeep. Operation "Varsity" had been a complete success: all objectives had been achieved despite some heavy losses, contact had been made with the ground forces, the enemy was disorganized and the Allies were ready to move out of the bridgehead and advance into the heart of Germany to finish the war. The next day the 6th Airborne Division headed towards the Baltic with the British VIIIth Corps, and the US 17th Division moved into the Ruhr to help in clearing the last German resistance.

PERFORMANCE

"Varsity" was the largest airlift of the war at that time. Two full airborne divisions had been lifted in one go within 2.5hr. But was "Varsity" necessary? It has been suggested that ground troops could have done the job as quick with fewer losses. There had been a high number of casualties on the first day, both in the air and on the ground—the open grassland of many of the DZs meant that there had been little cover for

Left and Right: A British Commando patrol rounding up snipers in the ruins of Wesel. The town had been devastated in a heavy attack by RAF Bomber Command at the start of the operation.

Below: An official photograph showing victorious British Commandos—one sporting a *Pickelhaube*!—resting in a ruined building in Wesel. The Commandos had formed the spearhead of the ground offensive, and had taken the town within hours of their crossing of the river.

the landing troops and the wounded. The British 6th Airborne Division lost 347 dead, 731 wounded, and 313 missing; RAF Nos 38 and 46 Groups lost 23 aircrew; the Glider Pilot Regiment lost 173 men killed or missing and 77 wounded (this figure is much higher than the American equivalent, probably because the British glider release height was much higher). American casualties were just as high: the 17th Airborne Division lost 393 dead, 834 wounded, and 80 missing; IXth Troop Carrier Command lost 169 aircrew killed or missing and 116 wounded, with 35 glider pilots killed.

However, German losses were even higher. It is estimated that the enemy lost virtually all of the 4,000-strong 84th Infantry Division killed, wounded or taken prisoner, plus large amount of artillery and guns which may well have delayed the Allied advance from the Rhine into Germany. Operation "Varsity" had been fast— the first bridge over the Rhine for the massed Allied armies on the west bank was completed by 16.30hrs and the high ground of the Diersfordter Wald which dominated the river crossing area and could have seriously hindered the crossing had been quickly made safe. The fact that the war was over six weeks later was proof of the success of the operation.

"ECLIPSE" & "EXODUS"

12 THE LIBERATION OF ALLIED PRISONERS OF WAR APRIL–MAY 1945

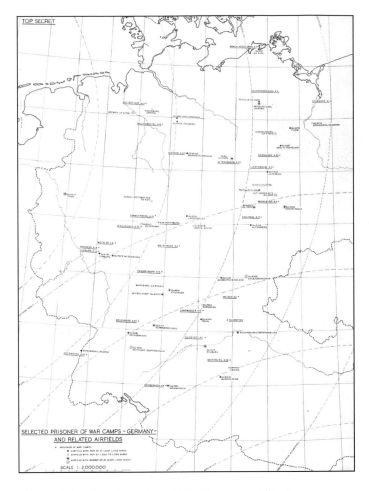

Above: Map showing selected POW camps within Germany and the most suitable airfields from which repatriation could take place, along with their runway lengths.

The cessation of hostilities in Europe saw a great mass of humanity on the move, about 750,000 people in the British Zone of Germany alone. There were displaced persons, refugees, and ex-prisoners of war—"kriegies," as they called themselves, from the German *Kriegsgefangener*.

For the British and American governments it was a crucial priority that their servicemen, who had been captured by the Germans, should be delivered home swiftly and safely, whatever the cost. Some of these men had not seen their families for five years. For the war-weary people being asked to carry on supporting the fighting in the Far East repatriation was, naturally, an emotionally charged matter For the governments concerned it was seen as a question of honor.

Within a week of the German surrender, on May 8, 1945, 130,000 of the total of 157,000 British and Commonwealth ex-POWs in the British Zone had been flown out of northwest Europe by Bomber Command and the USAAF in Lancasters, Halifaxes, and twin-engined Dakotas. This was the culmination of the RAF's great wartime enterprise. Air Marshal Saundby scribbled on the despatch of June 11 reporting on the airlift: "Undoubtedly a good show."

The remaining 27,000 men, mainly in Soviet hands, were repatriated later. Ex-POWs from the camps in eastern Europe, which were liberated by the Red Army, were taken to Odessa and then transported home by sea.

The sudden collapse of Germany meant that long-term repatriation plans had to be hastily revised. The original intention had been to set up staging and transit camps for the orderly evacuation of released men. This idea was now abandoned. A major part of Operation "Eclipse," which concerned itself with the care of POWs and plans for their repatriation, was the identification and selection of German airfields convenient to camps where ex-POWs could be collected and flown to Belgium and France and thence airlifted home. German rail-

ways were chronically disrupted and speed was essential to rescue the men from possible German reprisals; there was much talk of bands of roving "werewolves." At Stalag 357 in the village of Kittlitz (liberated May 2) the guards took away the prisoners' bedding and made them stand for long hours in the snow.

At the suggestion of AVM Bennet, Bomber Command took charge of the operation. At the end of September 1944 orders were given that heavy bomber aircraft and crews not needed for operations, or for immediate deployment against the Japanese, should be called upon to "assist in the maintenance and/or evacuation of Allied prisoners of war." It was the obvious solution to make use of the numbers of available aircraft and pilots used to the trip. A Lancaster or Halifax could carry between 20 and 24 men. Accordingly a Lancaster, a Halifax, a Stirling

ALLIED PHOTO RECONNAISSANCE

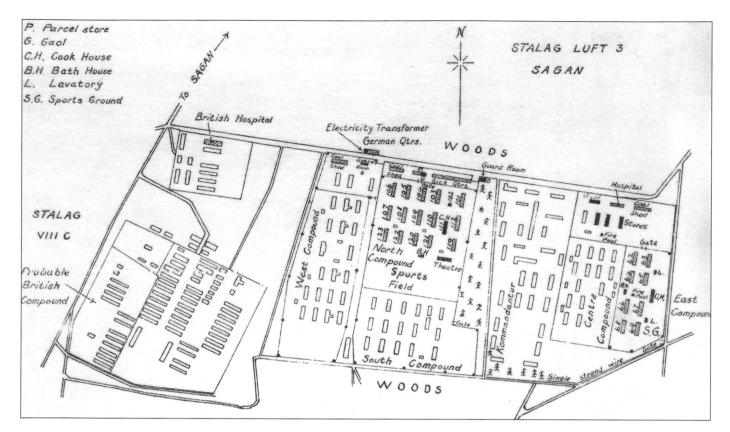

P. Parcel store
G. Gaol
C.H. Cook House
B.H. Bath House
L. Lavatory
S.G. Sports Ground

STALAG LUFT 3
SAGAN

British Hospital

Electricity Transformer
German Qtrs.

WOODS

STALAG
VIII C

Probable
British
Compound

West Compound

North Compound
Sports Field

Guard Room

Hospital

Coal Shed
Stores

Fire Pool

Gate

Theatre

Kommandantur

Centre Compound

East Compound

South Compound

WOODS

Single strand wire

Gate

and a Wellington were delivered to Netheravon for trials to be carried out by Transport Command in October and November.

Arthur Harris, RAF Commander-in-Chief, ordered immediate reconnaissance of all camps and the dropping of food and medical supplies. Wireless sets and ground panels were to be dropped by parachute, the panels to be accompanied by a code which would enable the prisoners to communicate with reconnaissance aircraft. Photographs already taken or acquired of camps were analysed. The International Committee of the Red Cross, which had access to most categories of camps, provided maps and photographs (some of which showed prisoners enjoying themselves—productions of *Aladdin* and the *Merchant of Venice*, sports days, and sailing model boats). POW camps were broadly divided into "Oflags" (short for *Offizierslager*) for officers and "Stalags" (*Stammlager*) for other ranks. The Luftwaffe had its own camps, the best known being Stalag Luft 3 at Sagan, of "Great Escape" fame.

An exercise in aerial reconnaissance was undertaken more to fill the gaps and facilitate the identification of suitable collection points. Nearly 30 German airfields were identified, with various runway lengths—of 1,700 yards, between 1,500 and 1,700 yards, and at least 1,500 yards—these lengths being critical for heavily loaded transports. Maps were plotted

Above and Below: Stalag Luft 3, at Sagan, is one of the best known of the prisoner of war camps, immortalized on film in the "Great Escape."

Bottom: Would-be escapers recaptured in January 1942. They were, at least, treated better than those recaptured from the Great Escape, many of whom were slaughtered.

P/W CAMP   ORANIENBURG
52° 46' N.   4081/51
13° 16' E.   (853489)
          Neg. No. 45041

STALAG LUFT I BARTH/VOGELSANG
54° 23' 00" N   4416/J7
12° 42' 00" E   232539
       A.C.I.U. Neg: No: 55066

Above Left and Right: Throughout the war, Allied PR missions had kept close watch on the POW camps to ensure that they were not hit during bombing raids and to ensure that Red Cross rules were followed. These photographs are of Oranienburg and Stalag Luft I at Barth/Vogelsang.

Right: British POWs housed in this factory in Brunswick, put markings on the roof in an attempt to protect it from attack—not easy when the bombing was by night and from high altitude!

showing their position vis-à-vis POW camps in the locality.

Camp after camp was liberated as the Allies advanced. In some cases prisoners were sent off by the Germans before Allied forces arrived; on April 18, Britain, France, and the United States accepted a German offer to leave all POWs where they were, near all fighting fronts. The combined forces of the Canadian First Army and British Second Army liberated Oflag 79 near Brunswick on April 12, the camp at Fallingbostel on April 16, Marlag and Milag Nord on April 28. The US Ninth, First, and Third Armies took the Lollar transit camp with POWs from Oflag XIIB (Handamar) on March 28, and then proceeded to Oflag XIIA/H, Pflag XIA/Z, Oflag VA, and Stalag XIIIC; the inmates from these last four camps had already been moved. Colditz (Oflag IVC) was liberated on April 15, Oflag VIIB on the 25th and Stalag

1–10. WATCH TOWERS.
11, 12. WATCH TOWERS (POSSIBLE).
13, 14. GATES.
15. GUARD QUARTERS (POSSIBLE).
16. COOK HOUSE.

TOWER 'A'   P/W QUARTERS   WALL   CELLS   GUARDS QUARTERS   TOWER 'B'

Above: Querum POW camp near Brunswick as seen on August 6, 1944.

Left and Below: Three views of the infamous Oflag IVC—better known as Colditz—that was liberated on April 15, 1945. Colditz has become the stuff of legend and the wonderful stories of its diehard escapers makes excellent reading.

P/W QUARTERS   TOWER 'A'

CHURCH   GUARDS QUARTERS   TOWER 'B'   P/W QUARTERS   TOWER 'A'

Left: Stalag VIIA at Moosburg on August 11, 1944. It would be liberated on April 29, 1945.

Below: As well as the joy of liberating POW camps there was the horror when the true depths of the depravity of the concentration camps were discovered. This photograph is of Belsen, which the British reached on April 15, 1945.

VIIA at Moosberg on the 29th. The prisoners down at Stalag XVIIIA at Wolfsberg, down near the Italian border had to wait for VE-Day.

The full extent of Nazi atrocities were revealed as the British and Americans entered the extermination camps on April 11, when the Americans liberated Buchenwald, four days later, the British reached Bergen Belsen; on the 29th the Americans got to Dachau. Richard Dimbelby's broadcast from Belsen and the photographs taken by the British Army team sent a "shudder of horror around the world."

Meanwhile, in many POW camps, Kriegies half mad with the joy of freedom went looting and raping as victors have since time began. In the woods around Stalag IVB at Königstein near Dresden, they hunted their hated captors down and Ordinary Seaman Gant remembered "bashing up Jerries, driving round in cars, eating, drinking and doing everything we wanted. The men were discouraged from going out, but started to cut holes in the fences and scrambled off to make whoopee. They found a barn of angora rabbits and killed and ate them. With hatchets and bayonets they butchered a band of 40 pigs and came back triumphant with great lumps of meat. Bicycles and milk floats and all sorts of strange vehicles were taken from the local town and a weird range of "souvenirs" acquired— climbing boots, ladies' feathered hats, and Tommy guns fished out of the river."

For the appalling skeletal remains of men who had been on the murderous death marches from the east, there was no energy left for exultant reprisals or crazy fun. Since early in the year the Germans had been withdrawing from the advance of the Red Army and had taken their prisoners of war with them. The inmates of Stalag XXB at Willenberg in Poland were route-marched through deep snow nearly 500 miles to Fallingbostel just north of Hanover. One of the doctors who stayed behind with the sick recalled the scene when, half an hour before midnight, on the bitter night of January 22, his fellow prisoners assembled ready to leave. Between eight and ten thousand souls, there were, he reckoned, of which two to three thousand were British, all pulling little sleds which they had hastily made to carry their few possessions and meager rations. In the dark, snowy hush he watched "endless columns of wretched men ambling away past the searchlights of the big main camp gates" and out into the night.

For three months they were marched, herded into fields to sleep with no fires, little food, no hot water and lashed by a bitter east wind. Those who could not keep up were shot; many died of starvation, hypothermia, or dysentery. The survivors reached the headquarters of Stalag

Right and Above: The extermination camp at Bergen Belsen in north Germany—the black open square (detail *Above*) is formed as the inmates undergo a roll call. Belsen at one time had 10,000 prisoners. It had no gas chambers: the inmates died from disease and starvation

Below Right: The POW camp at Oswiecim, with—unmarked— the extermination camps of Auschwitz and Birkenau.

P/W CAMP   OSWIECIM
1. 50°01.8'N   4081/128
   19° 12.2'E   (867446)
2. 50° 01'N   4081/128
   19° 17.7'E   (928447)
   Neg. N° 42594

XIB at Fallingbostel at the end of March. Charles Wilmot, the American war correspondent, was on the scene soon after the 7th Armoured Division took the camp (on April 16): "I saw them in hospital—drawn, haggard, starved—starved beyond description, limbs like matchsticks, bodies shrunken till their bones stood out like knuckles." Two days after liberation the men were flown out.

The great airlift (Operation "Exodus") had begun on Easter Tuesday (April 3). For days before armies of ragged men had been converging at the airfields marked out by the earlier PR flights thoughout Germany, and the main reception centers in Belgium and northern France. They came in "liberated" jeeps, lorries, battered old wagons, horse-drawn carts, fire engines, steam rollers; some rode bicycles. Dakotas were used to fly the men in from the scattered airfields to Brussels, Halle, and Rheims, where they were met by PWX staff and Red Cross representatives. From there they were flown to England in Lancasters and Halifaxes. For most Americans there was a long sea trip from Le Havre.

The men from Stalag VIIA had left Moosberg in lorries just three days after the Americans arrived, taking a long and circuitous route to Regensburg because so many bridges had been destroyed. The men stood waiting at the aerodrome, watching as Dakotas came and went, waiting their turn. Take-off was a chancy business as there was so little room on the bomb-pitted runway and some of the American pilots were "larking about," staying on the ground for what seemed much too long and then suddenly making a steep climb at the last moment.

It was at Oakley near Oxford that the very first batch of POWs arrived on the first day of "Exodus"—400 officers and NCOs from Oflag XIIB at Hadamar near Frankfurt. Five weeks later (May 8) the loudspeakers at Westscott Base boomed out: "We have now completed the landing of our 30,000th ex-prisoner of war at this station. Well done boys and girls! Let 'em all come!" And they all came. Between May 9 and May 15, 1945, an average of 3,568 ex-POWs were airlifted out of Juvincourt daily in about 146 aircraft—a total of 40,000 POWs in 1,600 aircraft. The Commanding Officer, Wg Cdr Elliott, was commended for his "tact in dealing with the Americans"—the airfield was under the command of an American colonel whose squadron was using the runway frequently.

Reception centers were established at Chalfont St Giles, Cosford, Amersham, Beaconsfield, Horsham, Portsmouth, and 20 or more other centers in the Midlands. Here the men were kitted out with new uniforms, with special attention being paid to medal ribbons, given pay, and railway warrants. Relatives were notified and as quickly as may be they were off home at last, for six weeks leave.

On May 6 Bomber Harris sent the following message to Nos 1, 3, 5, 6, 8, and 92 Groups: "Operation 'Exodus' is now proceeding and may be expected to continue for some time. The loads carried are of priceless value. The safety of returning POWs is of first importance . . . I know that all group commanders will understand this but I ask them to devote their personal attention to it." There were, however, a few accidents; some exhausted pilots failed to make it home, one, with a cruel irony, crashing his plane into the white cliffs of Dover.

But Operation "Exodus" was generally acclaimed as a tremendous success. Gen Eisenhower wrote to "Bomber" Harris on June 15 of "an achievement of great magnitude, comparable to the remarkable results of the offensive was waged by Bomber Command . . . please convey to all you air and ground crews, who took part, and particularly to those who worked so hard at airfields at Rheims and Brussels, my sincere compliments and thanks. It was a contribution to human happiness of which the Air Force can remain forever proud."

Repatriation was far less smooth for the 68,000 British Commonwealth subjects estimated to be in camps in Poland and Eastern Germany,

Left: The liberation of the camps was an essential but soul-destroying task once the extermination camps were reached. The incensed soldiers often forced guards—and even local townspeople—to help them with the cleaning up.

1-8. WATCH TOWERS.
9-11. GATES.
12, 13. SPORTS GROUNDS.
14, 15. POSSIBLE GUARDS' QUARTERS.

which had been overrun by the Soviets. There the prisoners had, it seems, passed from one form of captivity to another and many genuinely believed they had become prisoners of the Russians. A witness at the liberation of Stalag IVB wrote: "Four Ruskies on horseback ride into camp armed with Tommy-guns, pistols ,and hand grenades—bare-backed riders like brigands."

"It is obvious," wrote another, "that the Ruskies want to get rid of us."

British prisoners in the camp at Luckenwalde, south of Berlin, were kept, as were many others, as hostages until the return of Russians who had been liberated by the British. One of the 16,000 inmates, Flt Lt Barber, wrote: "If the government had refused to return the Russians, I do not doubt that most of us would have accepted our unhappy lot as being necessary consequence of the aftermath of war."

For these ex-POWs it was to be a long haul home. The Russians insisted that they should not be airlifted, but put on board ship at Odessa. Points of concentration were established at Lvov and Volkovsk. A team of British contact officers, sent in to prepare for the evacuation of prisoners, was only allowed in for 16 days. No access was allowed at all to the camps in Poland as the Soviets feared that contact might be made with the Polish leaders. Such was the harsh treatment meted out by the Russians that many men "went to ground" and took refuge with Polish families.

Above and Above Right: Stalag XIB at Fallingbostel as seen on March 29, 1944. (The photograph at right joins the other at its top right corner.) Some of the inmates liberated on April 17, 1945, had marched 500 miles from Poland in extreme conditions.

Below Right: Dachau, taken on September 18, 1941, showing its proximity to the town.

Detailed arrangements were made by the terms of the Yalta Agreement, signed by the British and Soviet powers on February 11, whereby each ally was to care for each other's nationals and organize transport. In the event, the Russians were unable to provide transport or accommodation; notices were simply pinned up instructing men to report to Odessa.

The "Kriegies" got home, most of them, to the delights of white bread, chocolate, alcohol, clean clothes, and their loved ones Not all were ecstatic; for some, coming back to the responsibilities and grind of work and family life, there was a strange lingering nostalgia not, perhaps for camp life, but for the first few heady weeks of glorious new freedom. Sergeant Wood from Stalag XIB looked back on those day as the best; he recalled "the pleasure we once found in lunching with Hungarian transport soldiers . . . the exhilaration of hunting food and wine, and found even their taste was fading. Somehow, although it was still May, an autumnal melancholy drifted in the mid-day dust."

ALLIED PHOTO RECONNAISSANCE

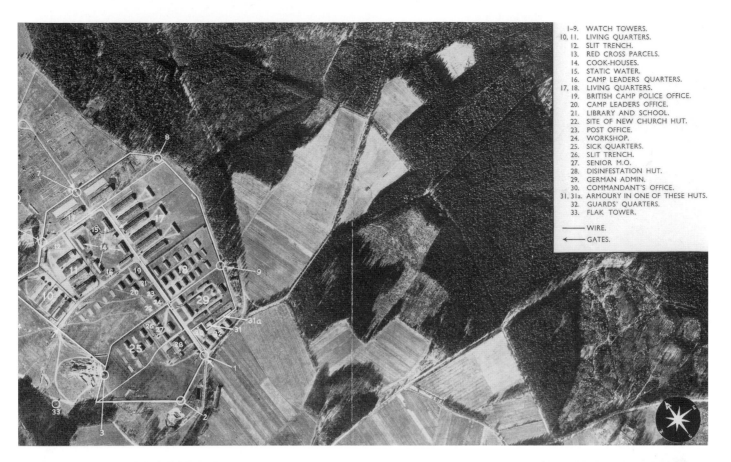

1-9. WATCH TOWERS.
10, 11. LIVING QUARTERS.
12. SLIT TRENCH.
13. RED CROSS PARCELS.
14. COOK-HOUSES.
15. STATIC WATER.
16. CAMP LEADERS QUARTERS.
17, 18. LIVING QUARTERS.
19. BRITISH CAMP POLICE OFFICE.
20. CAMP LEADERS OFFICE.
21. LIBRARY AND SCHOOL.
22. SITE OF NEW CHURCH HUT.
23. POST OFFICE.
24. WORKSHOP.
25. SICK QUARTERS.
26. SLIT TRENCH.
27. SENIOR M.O.
28. DISINFESTATION HUT.
29. GERMAN ADMIN.
30. COMMANDANT'S OFFICE.
31, 31a. ARMOURY IN ONE OF THESE HUTS.
32. GUARDS' QUARTERS.
33. FLAK TOWER.

——— WIRE.
←——— GATES.

OPERATIONS "ECLIPSE" & "EXODUS"

137

CONCLUSION

Allied PR capabilities at the outbreak of the war were a pale shadow of what was actually required. Despite the obvious lessons to be gleaned from World War I, and inter-war conflicts in China and Spain, neither British nor US defense chiefs attributed sufficient time or resources to creating an effective PR force. In 1939 the RAF possessed few officers or NCOs capable of the detailed analysis required if aerial reconnaissance was to be a strategic asset, and a motley collection of aircraft to perform this task. But for the energies of men such as Sidney Cotton—"the father of RAF PR"—and Grp Capt Fred Winterbotham, who did much to demonstrate to a reluctant Air Ministry the importance of PR, the quality of British aerial reconnaissance in the "dark days" of 1940-41 would have been seriously undermined.

The effects of inadequate reconnaissance were fatally demonstrated at Pearl Harbor. The USAAF entered the war in 1941 with a string of observation squadrons equipped with obsolete aircraft. The profound impact of the Japanese attack on Pearl Harbor in December 1941 invoked a huge shake-up in the American military. British intelligence had warned its American counterpart of the likelihood of a Japanese attack, based on information gleaned by PR pilots. In the aftermath, this fact was not altogether lost on American commanders. In the event the Pearl Harbor top brass tragically failed to heed the warnings. Nothing contributed more to the Japanese success than the lack of American long-range air reconnaissance. During the Congressional investigations, excuses were thick on the ground. The foremost among these was that with only 36 available aircraft, 360 degree searches would have been impossible. As with their British Allies, the Americans were quick to learn from their mistakes.

The Luftwaffe *Aufklärungsgruppe* v the Allies
Assessing the relative successes and failures of photo-reconnaissance are rather more difficult than in areas of air warfare, where results are immediately tangible. Generaloberst Werner

Below: In February 1943 a requirement for a standard installation of night cameras in all aircraft of Bomber Command was stated in a letter to the Air Ministry which said: ". . . one night photograph to be taken by each aircraft engaged on an operation, by a photoflash released by the first bomb (or a flare in the case of the Path Finder Force)."

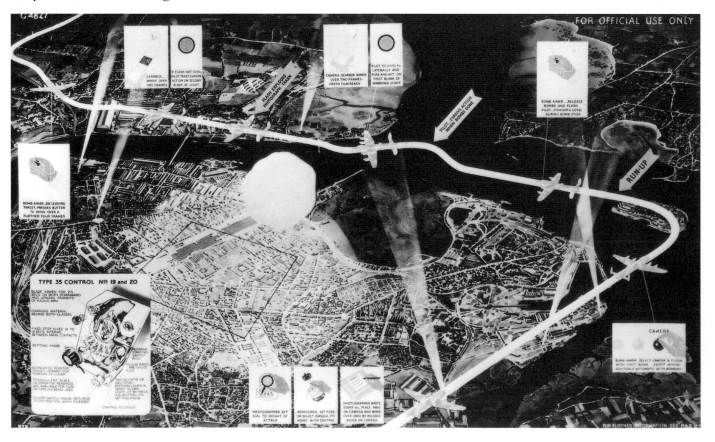

Left: Bomb bay camera view of two sticks of bombs dropping on Nuremburg—the bombs of the first stick are "jostling"; the target indicators of the second stick are dropping well.

Freiherr von Fritsch, a high-ranking member of the Wermacht planning staff, reported to the OKW in 1938 that "military organization which has the most efficient reconnaissance unit will win the next war." If that prophecy was indeed correct, then Allied PR played a vital role in the victory.

Perhaps the crucial difference between the Axis and Allied PR was that, while the Allies realized early in the war that fast, light, high-flying aircraft were the most suitable for the role, until 1944 both German and Japanese air forces persisted with converted bombers. Throughout this period the Luftwaffe proved singularly incapable of getting good PR coverage of the British Isles. At the outbreak of war in Europe, the special *Aufklärungsgruppe* (reconnaissance group) of the high command, under the experienced Oberst Theo Rowell, was a very capable and forward-looking unit with ambitious plans for long missions at altitudes above the reach of fighters.

As early as the fall of 1940, the Luftwaffe had a machine on its inventory that could fly to 42,000ft, well beyond the reach of any British fighter. The Junkers Ju 86P-2 was a pressurized version of an obsolescent bomber that first came into service in 1936. Despite its obsolescence in a bombing role, the Junkers was far more capable in the long-range reconnaissance role than anything in the RAF at this time.

The German aircraft industry continued to focus on developing high altitude long-range PR, aircraft in the face of considerable technical

hurdles. The development program for the ambitious Henschel Hs130 ran over time and over budget, and for four precious years the Luftwaffe were forced to rely on camera-equipped versions of its ordinary bombers, which were all highly vulnerable to both anti-aircraft fire and fighter interception. When it did come into service, the Hs130 was hampered by technical problems and was built in only limited numbers.

A far more formidable adversary was the Arado Ar234B-1, a high-altitude, twin-jet aircraft that came into service in September 1944. This technological marvel could fly at over 400mph at an altitude in excess of 32,000ft and was almost uninterceptable. These aircraft were finally able to provide the Luftwaffe and OKW with high-quality aerial photographs, but at a time when the war was already decided.

Whereas the RAF and USAAF had rapidly modernized their PR units to the demands of the war, the Luftwaffe wasted considerable time pursuing the development of the invulnerable PR platform. One of the greatest failures of the *Aufklärungsgruppe* was its failure to deliver accurate intelligence of the preparations for D-Day. The *Aufklärungsgruppe* made valuable missions over the Eastern Front, but only usually as a precursor to army units, to whom they were ultimately subservient.

Compare this with the successes of the fledgling Heston Unit. One of the first victories scored by the renamed No 2 Camouflage Unit, which became Photographic Development Unit in January 1940, was photographing the German invasion fleet prior to the assault on Norway in April 1940. Flying a specially modified Spitfire, Sqn Ldr Maurice Longbottom provided invaluable photographic evidence of the planned attack. This mission helped to prove the worth of using high-speed, single-seat aircraft for tactical photo-reconnaissance. In May 1940 Churchill made special mention of the importance he attached to aerial reconnaissance. In a few short months, the RAF woke up to the role of PR in modern warfare and made swift amends for their pre-war indifference. The introduction of aircraft such as the de Havilland

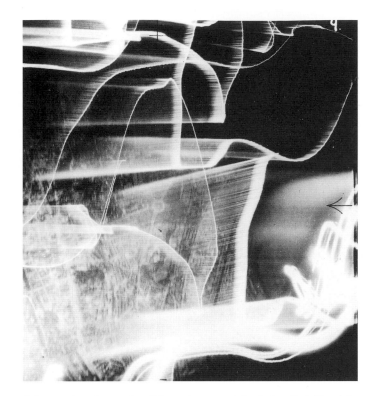

Mosquito into the PR role provided the RAF with a highly capable and reliable weapon in the PR war at a time when it most mattered, a point that is, perhaps, not lost on history.

RAF PR—Unarmed and alone

The PRU was chopped and changed and relocated, but continued to provide the Chiefs of Staff with intelligence during the years when Britain stood alone against the Axis. The location and tracking of the German super-battleships, accurate assessment of the invasion fleet that stood across the Channel in the summer of 1940, early warning of the invasion of Norway—all were largely achievements of reconnaissance pilots.

It would not be an exaggeration to say that the success of the Allied invasion of Sicily in 1943 can also largely be attributed to the accuracy of RAF PR. Several months before the planned invasion, a young RAF flight officer was scanning a print that showed a large merchant ship lying damaged on the bottom of Tripoli's shallow harbor. Looking closer Flt Off Humphreys noticed a tiny speck of white next to the ship, a mere pinprick on the print. From this he was able to assess accurately that the Italians were attempting to refloat the ship and use it to block the harbor entrance. Bomber raids were launched and succeeded in re-sinking the ship. Convoys of supply ships were then able to dock successfully when Tripoli fell on January 23, 1943, and unload cargoes vital to the Eighth Army's role in the invasion of Sicily. This was just one example of the persistent and highly effective role of the interpreters. Had Humphreys failed to notice the tell-tale wash of the bilge-pumps, the invasion of Sicily may well have been delayed.

The USAAF reconnaissance groups

Reports filtering back from the North African and Pacific campaigns during late 1942 and early 1943 made the USAAF realize that its outdated theories about observation tactics and aircraft were no longer valid. This modern war was calling for fast, maneuverable fighter aircraft, flying photo-reconnaissance, tactical reconnaissance, and photomapping missions. Intensive training during 1942 and early 1943 vastly increased the strategic value of USAAF PR, particularly with regard to their assessment of the usefulness of precision bombing in Germany. Specific variants of the P-51 Mustang and P-38 Lightning—the F-5 and F-6—gave the USAAF a vastly increased capability to bring back PR of immediate tactical value during their campaigns in the Pacific and Northern France.

During the preparations for D-Day, a joint US/British unit, No 106 (PR) Group was set up to control and coordinate strategic reconnaissance for the invasion. Flying low-level "dicing" missions, USAAF P-51s and P-38s brought back countless invaluable images of German defenses around the Normandy beaches. To ensure success, it was necessary to destroy German early warning radar installations along the coast of France. These, too, were tenaciously sough out by the PR units.

Photographic Interpretation—Seeing the wood for the trees

Developed in conjunction with PRU, the RAF Photographic Interpretation Unit played an equally vital role in the intelligence war. Prior to the conflict, the number of RAF staff trained in this field could be counted on the fingers of one hand. The administration and equipment that supported this small staff was equally inadequate. A mountain of photographs was of no use without some means of understanding their significance. Interpretation was no easy task, for it involved analyzing minute detail on photographs taken in less than ideal conditions. Like all intelligence, PR needed rapid assessment to be of use to field commanders. With this in mind, the RAF PIU was organized to carry out its work in three phases. The first involved a preliminary report made almost immediately that the aircraft landed. The camera film was rapidly developed, and the pilot could, at this stage, add any observations he had made from the cockpit. Within 24 hours a more detailed report would be prepared that provided tactical intelligence based on previous missions. This gave planners the ability to assess enemy activity and to respond accordingly. The final report assessed the strategic value of this information, both to the RAF and Britain's allies. After Russia's entry into the war, a vital flow of information between Britain and her eastern ally began, fostered in person by Churchill. The PIU developed many innovative ways of analyzing the precious photographic intelligence brought back by the PRU. For example Sqn Ldr Claude Wavell, one of the RAF's most accomplished interpreters, invented a device for measuring the height of objects on the ground, based on the length of the shadows they cast.

The resources and skills of the American units proved a great asset to the war against the Axis. A lack of cooperation between the two sides perhaps hampered the effective strategic and tactical use of photo intelligence prior to the Normandy campaign. This was partly a result of different working practices, a natural reluctance for intelligence units to share information even when working toward a common aim, and the fact that Anglo-American cooperation was still in its infancy during the Italian and North African campaigns. The establishment of the Allied Central Interpretation Unit helped to remedy this situation and ensured a pooling of information. As the war progressed, this task became increasingly difficult as German forces became adept in the art of camouflage and concealment. Here, too, the insight and resourcefulness of the American interpreters came into its own, and undeniably helped to foreshorten the war in Europe, and end the suffering of the civilian population in England. The frantic hunt for V-2 and V-1 launch sites at Peenemünde and on the western coast of France during 1944 required a huge collective effort that simply could not have been achieved without American photo-interpreters, many of them trained in England.

With the men and women of Government Code and Cypher School at Bletchley Park, the PIU provided the Chiefs of Staff with their most

Below: USAAF B-17s bomb the Fieseler aircraft factory at Kassel, July 30, 1943.

valuable source of intelligence during the desperate early months of the war. Working in conjunction with USAAF interpreters at the Allied Central Interpretation Unit, this vital stream of intelligence continued to play a central role in the decisions made by the Joint Chiefs of Staff until the end of the conflict.

The Strategic Bombing Offensive

The value of PR to the Strategic Bombing Offensive is harder to gauge, and proved to be a source of great contention. In fall of 1940, Bomber Command chiefs began to exhibit their irritation that the upstarts of the PIU were suggesting that their raids were largely ineffective. Heavy losses during daylight raids forced Bomber Command to concentrate on night bombing, but their pilots were poorly trained in this role, and lacked either accurate bomb sights or navigational aids. The eyes of PR units did not lie. They were able to show that the vast majority of British bombs were simply failing to hit their targets. In February 1942, Air Marshal

Arthur Harris became head of Bomber Command. Harris was an enthusiastic and determined advocate of area a bombing, a less discriminating tactic entirely.

Throughout April and May, Harris launched mass raids against poorly defended towns of limited strategic value. Photographic evidence proved that these raids were having little effect on the German war machine. The arrival of the US bomber groups in the European theater placed a great emphasis on the role of PR in assessing war damage. While the B-17s focused on precision daylight bombing, the RAF continued its night raids.

Although accuracy improved to some degree, Bomber Command pursued the policy of area bombing until the last months of the war. Harris eventually saw the merits of photographic interpretation, but at a time when the Germans had became wise to the technique of the PIU men and women. The Germans made extensive use of camouflage and decoying to mislead RAF pilots, and here, too, the bomber barons failed to make an accurate appreciation of PR. The Decoy Section at Medmenham was discounted on a number of occasions when its interpreters tried

Below: Merville airfield was attacked on September 15, 1943, by B-26s of 8th Air Force's 387th and 386th Bomb Group.

to show that false targets were being attacked. Pride, and a perceived need to defend the area bombing policy against criticism thus seriously hampered Bomber Command from making full use of RAF or USAAF PR for much of the war.

Above: Unique photograph of a German nightfighter in action on April 8/9, 1945. It has been illuminated by the photo-flash as the bombs are dropped.

Next Page: B-17s in action.

The role of PR in propaganda

Photographic evidence was widely used as a tool of propaganda during World War II. Press access to the photographs was, of course, strictly controled, but an undeniably important aspect of the PR war was the battle for the hearts and the minds of the civilian populations of Britain and the US. The heartening sight of the stricken *Tirpitz*, the pictures of the wholescale destruction of Hamburg and Dresden, and finally the explosions over Hiroshima and Nagasaki, all had a profound impact on the way that the war was perceived at home. The aerial photographs were skillfully utilized to provide evidence that the domestic war machine in the US and Britain was defeating the Axis. In the case of the bomber offensive over Germany this produced something of a mixed reaction amongst the population, and many were profoundly shocked and horrified by the power that was unleashed over

Japan. On the whole, however, the use of aerial photographs in the press may be seen as a successful exercise.

Of course, not all of the many hundreds of PR missions undertaken during the war met with success. Many met with tragedy. By November 1942, the chances of a pilot surviving an operational tour with a PR squadron in northwest Europe were estimated at no more than 31 percent. It took a particular type of bravery to fly alone, unarmed and very often underpowered aircraft over enemy territory to bring back photographic evidence. The men of British and American PR units showed exceptional courage and bravery in adverse conditions. Their sacrifice in one of the most undersung battles of World War II should not go unrecognized.

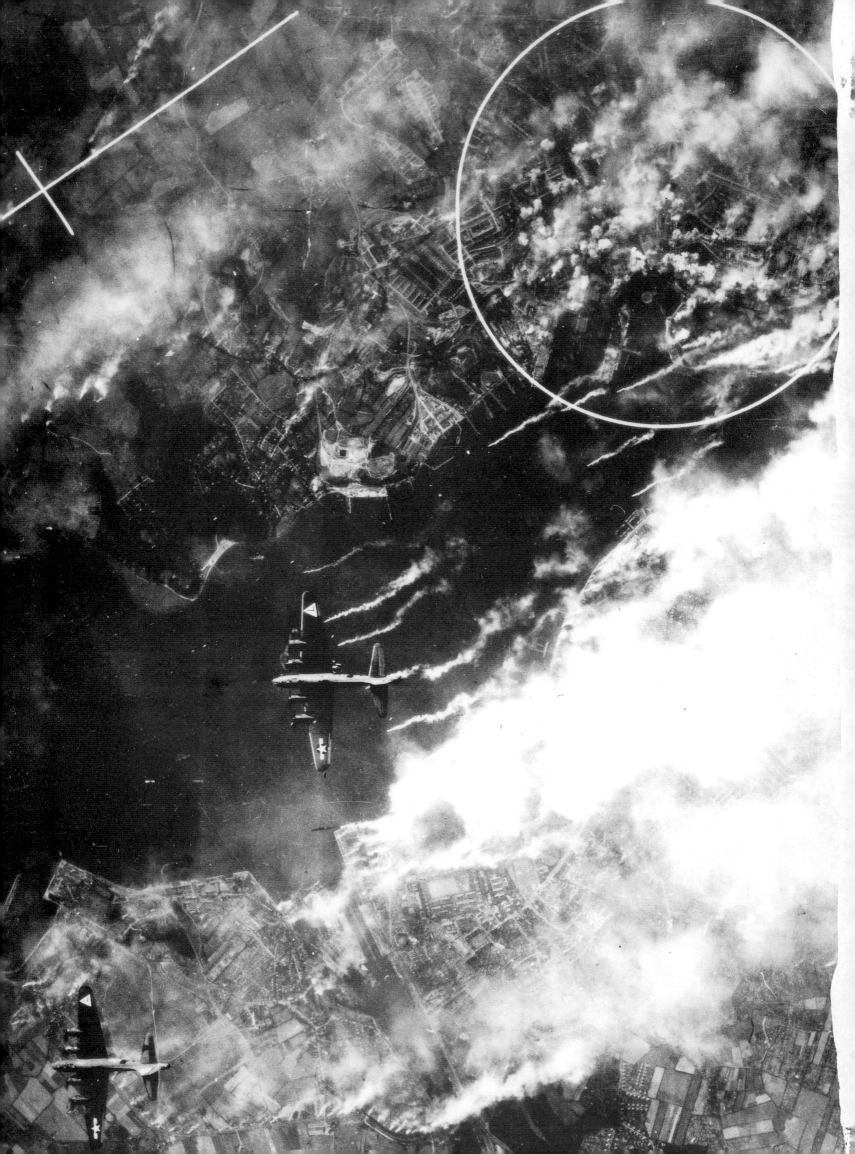